T0277589

Classical Greek Tragedy

Forms of Drama

Forms of Drama meets the need for accessible, mid-length volumes that offer undergraduate readers authoritative guides to the distinct forms of global drama. From classical tragedy to pantomime, pageant to performance art, the series equips readers with models and methodologies for analyzing a wide range of performance practices and engaging with these as 'craft'. Books follow a roughly three-part chronological structure and feature case studies providing exemplary close-up and detailed analysis.

SERIES EDITOR: SIMON SHEPHERD

Cabaret
978-1-3501-4025-7
William Grange

Pageant
978-1-3501-4451-4
Joan FitzPatrick Dean

Satire
978-1-3501-4007-3
Joel Schechter

Tragicomedy
978-1-3501-4430-9
Brean Hammond

Classical Greek Tragedy

Judith Fletcher

methuen | drama

LONDON • NEW YORK • OXFORD • NEW DELHI • SYDNEY

METHUEN DRAMA
Bloomsbury Publishing Plc
50 Bedford Square, London, WC1B 3DP, UK
1385 Broadway, New York, NY 10018, USA
29 Earlsfort Terrace, Dublin 2, Ireland

BLOOMSBURY, METHUEN DRAMA and the Methuen
Drama logo are trademarks of Bloomsbury Publishing Plc

First published in Great Britain 2022

ISBN: HB: 978-1-3501-4457-6
         PB: 978-1-3501-4456-9
         ePDF: 978-1-3501-4459-0
         eBook: 978-1-3501-4458-3

Series: Forms of Drama

Typeset by Integra Software Services Pvt. Ltd.
Printed and bound in India

To find out more about our authors and books visit www.bloomsbury.com
and sign up for our newsletters.

CONTENTS

FIGURES

SERIES PREFACE

The scope of this series is scripted aesthetic activity that works by means of personation.

Scripting is done in a wide variety of ways. It may, most obviously, be the more or less detailed written text familiar in the stage play of the Western tradition, which not only provides lines to be spoken but directions for speaking them. Or it may be a set of instructions, a structure or scenario, on the basis of which performers improvise, drawing, as they do so, on an already learnt repertoire of routines and responses. Or there may be nothing written, just sets of rules, arrangements and even speeches orally handed down over time. The effectiveness of such unwritten scripting can be seen in the behaviour of audiences, who, without reading a script, have learnt how to conduct themselves appropriately at the different activities they attend. For one of the key things that unwritten script specifies and assumes is the relationship between the various groups of participants, including the separation, or not, between doers and watchers.

What is scripted is specifically an aesthetic activity. That specification distinguishes drama from non-aesthetic activity using personation. Following the work of Erving Goffman in the mid-1950s, especially his book *The Presentation of Self in Everyday Life*, the social sciences have made us richly aware of the various ways in which human interactions are performed. Going shopping, for example, is a performance in that we present a version of ourselves in each encounter we make. We may indeed have changed our clothes before setting out. This, though, is a social performance.

The distinction between social performance and aesthetic activity is not clear-cut. The two sorts of practice overlap and mingle with one another. An activity may be more or less aesthetic, but the crucial distinguishing feature is the status of the aesthetic element. Going shopping may contain an aesthetic element – decisions about clothes and shoes to wear – but its purpose is not deliberately to make an aesthetic activity or to mark itself as different from everyday social life. The aesthetic element is not regarded as a general requirement. By contrast a courtroom trial may be seen as a social performance, in that it has an important social function, but it is at the same time extensively scripted, with prepared speeches, costumes and choreography. This scripted aesthetic element assists the social function in that it conveys a sense of more than everyday importance and authority to proceedings which can have life-changing impact. Unlike the activity of going shopping the aesthetic element here is not optional. Derived from tradition it is a required component that gives the specific identity to the activity.

It is defined as an activity in that, in a way different from a painting of Rembrandt's mother or a statue of Ramesses II, something is made to happen over time. And, unlike a symphony concert or firework display, that activity works by means of personation. Such personation may be done by imitating and interpreting – 'inhabiting' – other human beings, fictional or historical, and it may use the bodies of human performers or puppets. But it may also be done by a performer who produces a version of their own self, such as a stand-up comedian or court official on duty, or by a performer who, through doing the event, acquires a self with special status as with the *hijras* securing their sacredness by doing the ritual practice of *badhai*. Some people prefer to call many of these sorts of scripted aesthetic events not drama but cultural performance. But there are problems with this. First, such labelling tends to keep in place an old-fashioned idea of Western scholarship that drama, with its origins in ancient Greece, is a specifically European 'high' art. Everything outside it is then potentially, and damagingly, consigned to a domain which may be neither 'art' nor 'high'. Instead the European stage play and its like can best be regarded as a subset of the general category, distinct from the rest in that two groups of people come together in order specifically to present and watch a story being acted out by imitating other persons and settings. Thus the performance of a stage play in this tradition consists of two levels of activity using personation: the interaction of audience and performers and the interaction between characters in a fictional story.

The second problem with the category of cultural performance is that it downplays the significance and persistence of script, in all its varieties. With its roots in the traditional behaviours and beliefs of a society script gives specific instructions for the form – the materials, the structure and sequence – of the aesthetic activity, the drama. So too, as we have noted, script defines the relationships between those who are present in different capacities at the event.

It is only by attending to what is scripted, to the form of the drama, that we can best analyse its functions and pleasures. At its most simple analysis of form enables us to distinguish between different sorts of aesthetic activity. The masks used in *kathakali* look different from those used in *commedia dell'arte*. They are made of different materials, designs and colours. The roots of those differences lie in their separate cultural traditions and systems of living. For similar reasons the puppets of *karagoz* and *wayang* differ. But perhaps more importantly the attention to form provides a basis for exploring the operation and effects of a particular work. Those who regularly participate in and watch drama, of whatever sort, learn to recognize and remember the forms of what they see and hear. When one drama has family resemblances to another, in its organization and use of materials, structure and sequences, those who attend it develop expectations as to how it will – or indeed should – operate. It then becomes possible to specify how a particular work subverts, challenges or enhances these expectations.

Expectation doesn't only govern response to individual works, however. It can shape, indeed has shaped, assumptions about which dramas are worth studying. It is well established that Asia has ancient and rich dramatic traditions, from the Indian subcontinent to Japan, as does Europe, and these are studied with enthusiasm. But there is much less widespread activity, at least in Western universities, in relation to the traditions of, say, Africa, Latin America and the Middle East. Secondly, even within the recognized traditions, there are assumptions that some dramas are more 'artistic', or indeed more 'serious', 'higher' even, than others. Thus it may be assumed that *noh* or classical tragedy will require the sort of close attention to craft which is not necessary for mumming or *badhai*.

Both sets of assumptions here keep in place a system which allocates value. This series aims to counteract a discriminatory value system by ranging as widely as possible across world practices and by giving the same sort of attention to all the forms it features. Thus book-length studies of forms such as *al-halqa*, *hana keaka* and *ta'zieh* will appear in English for perhaps the first time. Those studies, just like those of *kathakali*, tragicomedy and the rest, will adopt the same basic approach. That approach consists of an historical overview of the development of a form combined with, indeed anchored in, detailed analysis of examples and case studies. One of the benefits of properly detailed analysis is that it can reveal the construction which gives a work the appearance of being serious, artistic and indeed 'high'.

What does that work of construction is script. This series is grounded in the idea that all forms of drama have script of some kind and that an understanding of drama, of any sort, has to include analysis of that script. In taking this approach books in this series again challenge an assumption which has in recent times governed the study of drama. Deriving from the supposed, but artificial, distinction between cultural performance and drama, many accounts of cultural performance ignore its scriptedness and assume that the proper way of studying it is simply to describe how its practitioners behave and what they make. This is useful enough, but to leave it at that is to produce something that looks like a form of lesser anthropology. The description of behaviours is only the first step in that it establishes what the script is. The next step is to analyse how the script and form work and how they create effect.

But it goes further than this. The close-up analyses of materials, structures and sequences – of scripted forms – show how they emerge from and connect deeply back into the modes of life and belief to which they are necessary. They tell us in short why, in any culture, the drama needs to be done. Thus by adopting the extended model of drama, and by approaching all dramas in the same way, the books in this series aim to tell us why, in all societies, the activities of scripted aesthetic personation – dramas – keep happening and need to keep happening.

I am grateful, as always, to Mick Wallis for helping me to think through these issues. Any clumsiness or stupidity is entirely my own.

Simon Shepherd

PREFACE

This book offers a comprehensive survey of the development of Classical Greek Tragedy in the context of ancient Greek social and political history during the Classical period (*c*. 480 to 404 BCE). It follows the tripartite chronological structure prescribed by the series with three case studies that provide detailed analyses of exemplary tragedies. I owe a debt of gratitude to Simon Shepherd for inviting me to participate in this project and for his guidance throughout. Thanks are also due to Lara Bateman and Mark Dudgeon for their editorial and administrative support, to Dharanivel Baskar for production support, and to my research assistant Mae Fernandes. Some of the research for this volume was made possible by funding from the Social Sciences and Humanities Research Council of Canada and by teaching relief provided by Wilfrid Laurier University. I am also grateful to Carolyn Cruthirds and the Boston Museum of Fine Arts, and the Parco Archeologico e Paesaggistico di Siracusa for providing images used in this book.

All translations from Greek tragedy are my own, unless otherwise indicated, and are based on the most authoritative editions of the texts. I refer to line numbers from specific plays, as is conventional, in round brackets. For fragmentary works of drama I refer to their catalogue number. References to other authors use the conventional reference numbers. In most instances when I transliterate ancient Greek terms I retain the inflected forms of the original.

1

Origins and Production

Classical Greek tragedy, an enduring and endlessly adaptable art form, is a product of the participatory democracy of fifth-century BCE Athens, although it was produced throughout the Mediterranean world. The literary texts that survive intact are scripts of dramas originally produced at state-sponsored festivals. There are thirty-two complete plays in all, representing only a fraction of the output of the three canonical tragedians, Aeschylus, Sophocles, and Euripides, in addition to numerous fragmentary texts, many by other dramatists. Titles and references to lost plays in later authors give some idea of the scope of the genre. Seven tragedies from Aeschylus, seven from Sophocles, and eighteen from Euripides survive.[1] These were produced in packages of three tragedies plus a shorter farcical satyr play at annual competitions honoring the god Dionysus (or in a package of two tragedies at a smaller festival, the Lenaea). This book will focus on one tragedy from each of the canonical trio in order to assess the development of the genre within its historical and social content over the fifth century: Aeschylus' *Seven Against Thebes*, Sophocles' *Oedipus Tyrannus*, and Euripides' *Helen*. These tragic poets were recognized as preeminent in the fourth century BCE, when copies of their texts were stored in public archives; the plays that survive come to us by means of medieval manuscripts based on that collection. Writing a history of tragedy is problematic for several reasons: the small representative sample out of several hundred productions, the lack of anything but fragments by other successful tragedians, the unknown dates of several surviving tragedies (although style and meter provide clues), doubts about the authenticity of portions of extant texts (including the endings of the three plays studied in this volume), the lost musical scores and choreography integral to their production, and the imperfect archaeology of the fifth-century theater of Dionysus, which was rebuilt *c.* 329 BCE, although some vestiges of the earlier theater remain (considered in detail by Goette 2007: 116–21).

Despite these daunting obstacles, some fundamental observations are possible. It is obvious that the genre went through a period of development in the first few decades of the century, followed by a robust and well-established *floruit.* Drama of the final decade retains its formulaic structure, but the role of the chorus is diminished, and the approach to subject matter in Euripides has a tendency toward self-reflexivity, skepticism, and iconoclasm. Although this assessment is based on a very limited sample, it is borne out, to a certain extent, by comments from the comic dramatist Aristophanes, who occasionally uses his medium to reflect on tragedy; Euripides is a favorite target. Aristophanes' *Frogs* features a contest between Aeschylus and Euripides in the afterlife in which each poet critiques the devices of the other, and thereby divulges some details of production. Further evidence, often terse or enigmatic, comes from Plato and Aristotle; the former bases his criticisms on a set of philosophical ideals, and the latter is at times frustratingly succinct, although his *Poetics* is a useful taxonomy of the elements of the genre. Later writers (for example the second-century CE scholar Pollux) had access to material lost to us; still, at times their conclusions seem questionable. The learned commentaries and marginalia included in medieval manuscripts provide further information. In addition, material culture is helpful. A few ceramic vessels produced in the fifth century supply details of production: the shape of masks, types of costumes and footwear, gestures of actors, and the musical accompaniment. These too have their limitations: there is a tendency for actors to "melt" into their mythological roles, making it difficult to ascertain when or if we are seeing details of a specific production. Additionally, a rich store of information regarding dates, titles, and victories in the contests comes from inscriptions, albeit fragmentary, including the so-called *Fasti*, a list of victories at the dramatic festivals that goes back as far as 501 BCE; votive monuments erected by *choregoi*, wealthy Athenians who sponsored tragic productions, celebrate specific victories.

We can be certain, however, that by 300 BCE classical tragedy was an artifact of nearly every Greek-speaking city-state in the Mediterranean world, as the remains of their theaters attest. The dramas were translated and adapted by the Romans, and became a staple of educational systems in late antiquity. Its exiguous remains, preserved in the Middle Ages, were formally revived in 1585 CE with the production of *Oedipus Tyrannus* in Vicenza, Italy, at the Teatro Olimpico, a replica of those early theaters. Although subsequent productions were rare until the nineteenth century, tragedy has survived as one of the most admired literary products of the ancient world. (See Burian 1997 and Garland 2004 for its historical reception.) Yet while the genre's prestige and influence since the fifth century are obvious, its early history is less so.

Early Development

Evidence for the origin of tragedy is fragmentary and from different periods; none of it is conclusive. Even the term "tragedy" is debated, although "goat song," a reference to a notional early prize, seems as good a theory as any.[2] Some form of drama must have existed, most likely in a ritual context, in Athens before the classical period. Several ceramic vessels from the sixth century BCE depict processions suggestive of early versions of the parade that launched the

Athenian festival of Dionysus. Aristotle's *Poetics* (1449a: 10–15), the earliest textual evidence for tragedy's origins, tells of its "improvisational beginning from those who lead off the dithyramb" (a choral hymn), an action that might be discerned on the aforementioned pots (Csapo and Wilson 2014: 927–8). Nonetheless, although the festival honoring Dionysus was instituted earlier (528), the *Fasti* listing winners of the tragic competitions only go back as far as 501 BCE.

Poetics was written around 320 BCE, several decades after the final surviving tragedy was produced, although the genre still flourished well into the fourth century. The concise style of the treatise indicates that it was not meant for publication (scholars suggest it served as lecture notes), and parts may be by other authors. Even so, it provides a starting point by associating the development of tragedy with the dithyramb, a choral song still performed during the classical period at the same festivals as tragedy. Drama came into being, the theory goes, when one member of the chorus assumed a speaking role. Later sources name Thespis as the first actor/producer of tragedy, the first to use masks to create a dramatic identity, and winner of the first dramatic competition and its goat prize in 534 BCE. The Roman poet Horace (*Ars Poetica* 275–7, *c*.19 CE) credits Thespis with taking his plays on tour in wagons throughout Attica (the rural area around Athens) and staining his troupe's faces with wine lees. Yet based on the lists of early victories in the tragic competition (the *Fasti*), Martin West (1989) has challenged these notions, thus supporting the contentions of Sir Arthur Pickard-Cambridge in his magisterial work on the Athenian dramatic festivals (1966: 72) that none of the fragments assigned to Thespis are genuine.

Aristotle observes that tragedy went through many changes until it reached its "true nature," and while there is not much we can say about the formative stages of the genre, there is evidence of the nature of its early fifth-century productions. As we know, by at least the beginning of the century tragic drama had been incorporated as a competition in the City Dionysia (discussed in more detail below), one of the largest religious festivals in Athens; a temple of Dionysus and adjacent theater were also built around this time. The names of some early tragedians and titles of their plays are recorded in the *Fasti* and elsewhere; a few fragments (citations in later authors) survive.[3] Phrynichus, the most renowned, produced *The Capture of Miletus* in 490 based on a historical event: the Persians' complete annihilation in 494 of a Greek city with close connections to Athens, on the coast of Asia Minor. According to the historian Herodotus (6.21), it was so heart-breaking that the Athenians imposed a hefty fine on the poet. (This would have been decided in a democratic assembly held in the theater after the festival to review the conduct of its participants.) Titles preserved for Phrynichus indicate that he otherwise dealt with the mythical corpus that provided plots for surviving tragedies; for example his *Daughters of Danaus* would have treated the infamous husband-killing women introduced in Aeschylus' *Suppliant Women*. According to the *Suda* (a Byzantine encyclopedia compiled in the tenth century CE), Phrynichus was responsible for introducing female characters (always played by male actors) into tragic plots. If this is true, it was an important innovation with a profound effect on the development of the genre, expanding the scope of its subject matter. While the *Suda* is not the most reliable source, the assertion may reflect Phrynichus' powerful female characters (Wright 2016: 18); certainly all three of the canonical tragedians featured redoubtable women including Clytemnestra, Antigone, and Medea. Among surviving tragedies only Sophocles' *Philoctetes* (409 BCE) does not have any female roles.

In 472 Aeschylus paid homage to Phrynichus' *Capture of Miletus* with a quote in his *Persians*, the oldest surviving Greek tragedy.[4] *Persians* also deals with a historical event—it is exceptional among surviving tragedies in this respect. The other two plays of the trilogy had mythological themes, with a satyr drama entitled *Prometheus* at the end, as we know from the *hypothesis*, a summary included in the manuscript tradition. The combination of historical and mythical subjects might have been unusual in its day, although we know so very little about early tragic trilogies. The defeat of the Persian invasion at the battle of Salamis in 480 is presented from the perspective of the failed king Xerxes as he returns home to a chorus of elders and his mother in Susa. *Persians* requires only two actors, who would have divided the roles between them; the text gives no evidence that the *skene* building, which represented various interiors in later plays, was used.

Despite its position as an example of early drama, *Persians* demonstrates a nuanced appraisal of the human condition apparent in later tragedy, including Sophocles' *Oedipus*, discussed in this volume. While some scholars have been content to assess the play as an exponent of the dangers of *hubris*, A. F. Garvie (2008: xxiii–xxxiii, the most recent scholarly edition of the play) observes that this interpretation is not evident in the text.[5] Far from being an example of patriotic *Schadenfreude* (the stirring descriptions of the Greek naval victory at Salamis notwithstanding), *Persians* treats Xerxes' downfall as a complex blend of human error and divine will. Aristotle's *Poetics* disapproves of tragic plots that treat the downfall of utterly base characters, and Aeschylus' Xerxes, who had tried to emulate the success of his father Darius, is notable for both his patriotism and his failure. Like Aeschylus' *Agamemnon* and Sophocles' *Oedipus*, for example, this drama outlines a trajectory from the protagonist's great prosperity to his utter ruin; like those mythical heroes, Xerxes must negotiate a world in which the inscrutable designs of the gods are only evident after the catastrophe has occurred. All things considered, *Persians* offers a deeply reflective and complex view of the world. It seems that even as tragic drama was in its formative stages the genre was capable of articulating difficult questions about the limits of human endeavor.

Aeschylus' earliest surviving tragedy is an example of his dramaturgical virtuosity. Its chorus of Persian elders, following instructions from their queen, summons the ghost of King Darius, who manifests to offer advice and upbraid his son Xerxes for losing the battle of Salamis. Even through the imperfect lens of our text, which offers no explicit directions about staging, we can envision the stunning effect of the lavishly costumed elders—Persians had a reputation for luxurious apparel—and the appearance of their esteemed, but departed, king. There is evidence to suggest that such ghostly apparitions were an established feature of early tragedy. J. R. Green (1994: 17–18) interprets a vase produced in Athens *c.* 490 (now in Basel, BS 415) as a chorus of youths summoning a ghost from a tomb. (The interpretation is not universally accepted; see Wiles 2007: 18–19.) Pollux writes of a tunnel that opened in the performance area, "the steps of Charon," from which such ghosts could make their appearances.

Upon examination of this earliest specimen of tragedy, we observe several similarities with Aeschylus' *Seven Against Thebes*, to be treated in detail shortly. But *Persians* has distinctive features that invite speculations about the development of the genre. It lacks a prologue, which, according to Aristotle's definition, is the part of the play before the entrance of the chorus. The action begins with the arrival of the Persian elders chanting in the "marching" anapestic meter. This is not necessarily typical of early tragedy, since various sources mention the prologues of Phrynichus (Garvie 2008: 43), but there are no extant examples of the absent prologue in later tragedy. As Garvie notes, there is evidence of the phenomenon in other early plays: Aeschylus' (lost) *Myrmidons* also began with the entrance of the chorus. We may conclude that both ways of launching a drama were possible in the early stages of the genre. Eventually, however, the prologue became the regular means of starting a tragedy. In *Persians*, its absence helps to establish the chorus as an important constituent of the dramatic scope. They personify Persia itself and the military disaster is their own ruin. The play is predominantly choral lyric. Comparing this with Euripides' *Orestes* (408 BCE) in which choral songs constitute only 10 percent of the text, and with other later plays, we might conclude that the role of the chorus diminished as the genre developed. However, a fresh analysis by Lucy Jackson (2020) suggests that the chorus was a much more vital element in fourth-century tragedy that previously believed.

The crucial presence of the chorus, a seminal component of the genre, is especially pronounced in Aeschylus' *Suppliant Women*, where it represents the daughters of Danaus as they flee marriage with their Egyptian cousins and seek sanctuary in Argos, mother-city of their ancestor Io. Like *Persians*, it begins with the advent of the chorus, which remains the center of attention, and whose lyrics comprise more than half the drama. As with *Persians* and *Seven Against Thebes* the speaking roles would be divided between two actors, but unlike those plays these roles do not hinge on complex moral choices. The protagonist, or principal actor, would play the girls' father, Danaus, whose role is to keep his obstreperous daughters in line (for example, they threaten to hang themselves on the city's altars if they do not get the sanctuary they demand). But the theory that the enhanced role of the chorus is evidence of tragedy's earliest form was demolished with the discovery of a papyrus scrap that dates it to 463 BCE, later than previously believed (Garvie 2006: ix–xxii). In other words, it was produced after *Persians* and *Seven Against Thebes*, neither of which gives such a prominent role to the chorus. Alan H. Sommerstein (2010: 109) suggests that Aeschylus was attempting something "very unusual" in making the chorus a character in the play, but the poet was working with a myth that allowed him to do this.

Even with significant gaps in our knowledge of early theater, or at least early Aeschylus, we can conclude that while tragic drama had a consistent formal structure—a series of episodes divided by choral songs and dance, dialogue in iambic trimeter, a tetralogy format (three tragedies and a satyr play)—the genre was flexible and innovative. Aeschylus manipulated the resources at his disposal with ingenuity and skill, as these early plays reveal. But in order to appreciate what Aeschylus, and indeed all tragedians, accomplished with those resources, we must look more closely at the performance conditions of tragedy in fifth-century Athens.

The Physical Space

Tragedy was by no means an elitist art form; at different stages of its existence admission was either free or subsidized. Thousands of spectators shared what Richard Schechner (1977: 160–2) describes as a "sociometric" space with actors and chorus. The open-air theater at the foot of the Acropolis was surrounded by the city visible to its audience, since all productions were in daylight. Spectators and performers were united by the devotional purpose of theater and its civic context. The watchers and the doers in the theater, as Gaye McAuley (2000) theorizes in her discussion of dramatic space, created "complex flows of energy between both groups," but unlike comedy the characters of tragedy never explicitly acknowledge the audience. Even so, prologue speeches and verbalized thoughts (asides) implicitly indicate an awareness of their presence (Bain 1977).

Although very early Athenian drama might have been performed in the agora, or central public area of the city, the purpose-built theater on the south slope of the Acropolis in the sanctuary of Dionysus *Eleutheros* ("the liberator") was the most important performance space in the city. It is generally accepted that all surviving Greek tragedy was composed for this venue; re-performances, at least from the fifth to third century, would have been in some facsimile of the theater of Dionysus in other locations. (The best discussion to date of the deme theaters is Csapo and Wilson 2020: 17–18). The stone theater in its current state (Figure 1), with a tiered semicircle of benches around a roughly circular paved surface, is not materially the same as that fifth-century theater, but it does occupy the same space and features the same general outlines. The fundamental components of this performance space are as follows:

(1) The *theatron* ("viewing space"), originally rows of wooden benches, had a capacity to hold thousands of spectators: according to Plato's estimate (*Symposium* 175c), audiences

Figure 1 *Stone theater of Dionysus, Athens, Greece. Courtesy Getty Images*

could be as large as 30,000, although modern calculations are more in the range of 4,000 (Csapo 2007: 27). As Schechner observes (1977: 162), the bench format, rather than individual seats, contributed to the communal nature of the experience. It is also quite likely that there was an unofficial audience space above the *theatron* where subaltern members of society could watch the production (Roselli 2011: 81).

(2) The *orchestra* (literally the "dancing place") was roughly 20 meters wide, which the chorus occupied. Its current shape in the Theater of Dionysus is curved, as are other stone theaters, for example, the beautifully preserved theater at Epidauros (Figure 2), which has remarkable acoustics and still hosts productions of ancient tragedies. The dithyrambic choruses, also part of the festivals, performed circle dances, which adds weight to the theory that the orchestra in Athens was circular. On the other hand, the very early stone theater at Thorikos (Figure 3), in rural Attica, is rectilinear, wider than it is deep, and some scholars (e.g., Goette 2007) argue for a rectangular

Figure 2 *Theater at Epidauros, Greece. Courtesy Getty Images*

Figure 3 *Theater at Thorikos, Greece. Courtesy Getty Images*

or trapezoidal orchestra in the Athenian theater. In any case, the term *orchestra* designates the space between the audience and the actors. The *thymele*, an altar of Dionysus, stood in its center. In addition to the chorus, and at times actors, an *auletes* (flute player) stood somewhere in the region of the *orchestra*.

(3) The "performance space" will be the term used throughout this book for the area occupied by the actors. Theater historians debate whether there was a raised stage beyond the orchestra, and if so when it came into existence. Neither archaeological nor textual data provide substantive evidence for the early part of the century, although there is speculation about its existence by the middle of the century (the evidence is assembled by Arnott 1962: 6–40). Some ceramic vases from Southern Italy, which had a flourishing performance culture, indicate a raised stage; these date from the fourth century and do not necessarily reflect Athenian architecture, even though Athenian plays were popular there. If there had been a stage in the fifth-century theater of Dionysus, it probably would have been quite low. In Euripides' *Helen*, for example, the actor apparently moves into the *orchestra* at certain points, which would have been cumbersome with a high raised stage.

(4) The *skene* building behind this space represented various interiors. The *skene*, (literally "hut"), which gives us the term "scene," was a wooden structure with a single set of doors, from which actors could enter or exit, and where they changed costumes and masks to become different characters. It could represent a palace (most frequently), a temple, a peasant's cottage, a cave, or whatever the story required. The texts of four early plays, all by Aeschylus (if we accept him as author of *Prometheus Bound*), give no indication that it was in use before the 450s, but his *Oresteia* trilogy (458 BCE) makes brilliant use of the *skene*, especially in *Agamemnon* where it is virtually a character in its own right, a brooding presence representing the violent family history of its main character. The captive priestess Cassandra envisions the ghosts of slaughtered children above it, before she enters to meet her own death. Clytemnestra slaughters Agamemnon, whose death cries are heard by the audience, within its walls. With one exception (Euripides' *Helen*, analyzed in the final chapter) the chorus does not enter the *skene*.

(5) Two *eisodoi*, long passageways leading to the *orchestra*, allowed the chorus and characters to enter from other outside places. According to the late writer Pollux, the left *eisodos* represented areas close at hand, while the right one led further afield. The problem with this observation is that we do not know whose left or right (the audience's or the actors') Pollux means. In all likelihood, there was a convention that allowed the audience to recognize from which direction a character was approaching.

Dramatic Festivals

The theater was sacred to Dionysus, a complex god of revelry and transformations. In Athens tragedy was performed at two yearly festivals, state-sponsored religious events, dedicated to him. In addition tragedies were re-performed in what have been termed "rural Dionysia" and in other cities from the early fifth century onward. The largest of these festivals, the Athenian City Dionysia, extended for five days and gave space and resources to three tragedians, who each produced a tetralogy (three tragedies and a satyr play). The selected three tragic poets were given a full day each for their productions. From 486 on, five comic playwrights produced a single comedy each, all on the same day, and dithyrambic choruses performed on the first day at the same event.[6] The festival took place in early March (the Athenian month *Elaphabolion*), when allies and other foreigners could travel by sea. Several months earlier, playwrights submitted a proposal to the Archon, the elected magistrate whose duties included overseeing the festival. Three authors were granted a chorus, financed by a wealthy citizen appointed by the state to fulfill the role of *choregos*. His obligations included the sustenance and training of the chorus who performed for all four plays, and the costumes and masks for all performers. The state contributed by funding the actors, at first two and then three. In tragedy's formative period the playwright would also act in his own plays, although Sophocles abandoned this practice, it is said, because of a weak voice. In addition, the playwright wrote the musical scores for his plays and the choreography. He could also take on the task of training his choruses; otherwise the *choregos* paid for the *chorodidaskalos* (trainer).

The role of this individual in tragic productions has been explored by Peter Wilson (2000), who situates the *choregos* in the democratic, yet fiercely competitive, ideology of Athens. Funding a tragedy provided opportunities for displays of wealth, albeit within the egalitarian context of a production before a mass audience. The *choreutae* (members of the chorus) were selected (we know not how) from the general population, many of whom had been trained in music and dance from an early age. John J. Winkler (1990), in a stimulating, but ultimately unprovable, argument, put forth the theory that they were ephebes, Athenian citizens-in-training, all around eighteen years old. Their performance in the chorus, according to his hypothesis, had "quasi-military features" that contributed to their training as warriors. Winkler offered as evidence the Pronomos vase, a rare depiction of a satyr chorus, whose members would have performed in all four plays (with four distinct collective personae) of a tragic production (Figure 4). The vase celebrated Pronomos, the *auletes*, or flute player, and commemorated a tragic victory. (A volume edited by Taplin and Wyles 2010 explores the vase in detail.) The *choreutae* are costumed but not wearing their masks, and we can see that they are beardless. Winkler argues their youthful energy gave them stamina enough to perform in all four plays, a physically demanding feat that included singing and dancing simultaneously. This controversial theory has not been widely accepted, and it is more likely that other factors contributed to a citizen's eligibility for performance in a chorus.

Prior to the festival an ancient wooden cult image of Dionysus was brought to the sanctuary in a procession. There was a preliminary event, the *Proagon* ("pre-contest"), at which the poet appeared with his actors (without masks or

Figure 4 *The Pronomos Vase (produced c. 400 BCE) depicting a satyr chorus, actors, and the auletes (flute player), Pronomos, who commissioned the piece. Courtesy Getty Images*

costumes) to describe his forthcoming production. At some point the competing poets drew lots to determine the day on which they would compete. Judges of the competition were selected from the citizen body, again by lot, on the first day of the City Dionysia. The festival, albeit a dedication to the god, had a pronounced civic flavor. For example, in the preliminary ceremonies the citizens being honored with public distinctions were announced. And during the period of Athens' imperial power, tributes from allies were displayed in the theater, and the orphans of the war dead were given special honors. The lesser festival, the Lenaea, also in honor of Dionysus, started to include dramatic competitions in the mid-fifth century, although there are fewer details about its administration; no surviving tragedies have been identified as Lenaean. (The data are scrutinized by Sourvinou Inwood 2003: 120–6.)

The Chorus

The chorus was, for an ancient audience, the *sine qua non* of Greek tragedy, and yet from our perspective it is the most difficult element to appreciate. Scholars such as David Ley emphasize its centrality. Ley (2007: 17) argues that the interaction between chorus and characters developed from the actor's essential function, which was to address the chorus, "the addressee of the characters almost constantly," an assertion illustrated by Aeschylus' *Seven*. And although later tragedy features animated conversations between two or three characters, the chorus usually expresses its opinion during these exchanges.

Two hundred years ago, the German scholar-poet August Wilhelm Schlegel (1846: 76–7) described the chorus as "the ideal spectator," an influential analysis that continues to hold, although with qualifications. Choruses often have less knowledge than spectators, and in many cases they represent marginalized members of society, a contrast to the heroic status of the characters. But it is difficult to make any generalizations about choral identity or their agency within tragic action. Aeschylus' choruses, even in his surviving plays, encompass a broad range of identities including Persian elders (*Persians*), African girls of Greek descent (*Suppliant Women*), and the demonic Furies (*Eumenides*). The latter two choruses are anything but marginal or passive. The daughters of Danaus in *Suppliant Women*, as noted earlier, function as the central character. The Furies pose a serious threat to Orestes that even the god Apollo cannot contain; they pursue the matricide to Athens and act as prosecutors in a trial; when he is exculpated they threaten to blight the land until Athena mollifies them with cultic honors.

As we have observed the *choregos* could hire a *chorodidaskolos*, but there is abundant evidence that the poet instructed his own choruses. According to a third-century CE author, Athenaeus (*Deipnosophistae* 22a), who is relying on earlier authors now lost to us, the early tragic dramatists Thespis, Pratinas, and Phrynichus "depended on the dancing of the chorus for interpretation of their plays." Athenaeus singles out Aeschylus for dispensing with choreographers and creating moves for the chorus. Very little can be stated with certainty about the appearance and movements of the tragic chorus; even the number of its members is up for debate. Pollux asserts that it originally comprised fifty members, was then reduced to twelve, and subsequently raised to fifteen. The chorus of Aeschylus' *Suppliant Women* represented the fifty daughters of Danaus, but was this the size of the dramatic chorus itself? Although scholars are skeptical that a tragic chorus ever had fifty members, most accept that it grew from twelve in Aeschylus' day and then increased to fifteen. Oliver Taplin (1978) disputes this, arguing that it always had fifteen members, while David Sansone (2016) argues that it was fixed at twelve choristers and that Pollux misinterpreted information that included the three actors, a later development of the genre. The most recent, and most authoritative, assessment (including inscriptional evidence) by Eric Csapo and Peter Wilson (2020: 16) establishes the number of choristers at fifteen by at least 440.

The following chapters will look in greater detail at the nature and function of the choruses of three representative tragedies. In every case they are inextricably part of the drama, although there are obvious differences between them. Modern productions of tragedy tend to truncate or omit their odes, but as we shall observe these songs not only add context and meaning to the action, but also help to modulate audiences' affective responses.

2

Early Tragedy: Aeschylus' *Seven Against Thebes*

In 467 BCE Aeschylus won first prize at the City Dionysia with a tetralogy focusing on the blighted royal family of Thebes, a dynasty whose mythology was well known to his audience from earlier epic poetry and art. *Seven Against Thebes*, the only extant drama of the package, was preceded by *Laius* and *Oedipus*, and followed by the satyr drama, *Sphinx*. It was, as Aristophanes put it (*Frogs* 1021), "full of Ares" (the god of war), a subject Aeschylus, who had fought against the Persians, knew well. And so did many members of his Athenian audience, whose citadel Persian invaders had sacked a decade before. The fear of attack that pervades the first part of *Seven* undoubtedly had a particular resonance for many spectators at its premiere. While the trauma of invasion is displaced onto a mythic Theban landscape, the play also interrogates the category of enemy. One brother, Polyneices, leads a contingent of foreign allies to attack his own city under the rule of another brother, Eteocles. The play opens as this violent event is about to take place. The two preceding tragedies, as their titles suggest, treated the family's history over several generations: the first, Laius, dealt with the father of Oedipus, the subject of the second play. We know very little about how Aeschylus handled this complicated family history, although the chorus of *Seven* gives a summary that links Oedipus' discovery of his incestuous marriage to his mother with his curse against his sons. It seems most likely that the preceding play provided more details. Aeschylus does not explain why Polyneices is marching against Thebes in *Seven*, although in other versions Eteocles reneged on an agreement to share the throne with his brother in alternate years. But poets were at liberty to shape a traditional story to fit their artistic vision. In the face of such mutable traditions there can be no certainty about Aeschylus' treatment of circumstances prior to Polyneices' invasion, although the traditional reason seems most likely. Even without full knowledge of the events dramatized in *Laius* and *Oedipus*, however, we can appreciate the urgency and emotional intensity that Aeschylus creates right from the opening lines. The following discussion, in addition to exploring how he accomplishes this, will serve as an introduction to the basic structure of tragedy, which remained consistent for the remainder of the century. It will also assess available information about staging and production features, still in their formative period.

Aeschylus and his contemporaries used the trilogy format to present a continuous narrative; later productions seem to favor three unconnected story lines. Euripides produced three plays dealing with the fall of Troy as a package in 415, one of which (*Trojan Women*) survives, but to judge from titles and fragments of the other two plays, it did not present the linked narrative of earlier trilogies. The only complete surviving trilogy is Aeschylus' *Oresteia*, which deals with the intrafamilial murders of another accursed dynasty, the house of Atreus. Agamemnon sacrifices his daughter, Iphigenia, to appease the goddess Artemis and get fair winds to Troy; his name-play focuses on his return to his angry wife Clytemnestra, who murders him in revenge. In *Libation Bearers* (also known as *Choephori*) her son Orestes requites his father's murder with matricide; and in *Eumenides* he is pursued by the avenging Furies of Clytemnestra until he is exculpated in the court of the Areopagus in Athens (Aeschylus' innovation to the tradition). The trilogy is unified not only by its linked stories, but also by the overarching theme of justice, which evolves from retributive violence to the institutionalized law court founded by the goddess Athena and additionally by a complex system of imagery. The lost satyr drama *Proteus* treated the adventures of Agamemnon's brother Menelaus as he made his way home with his wife Helen. While tragic poets continued to produce packages of three tragedies and a satyr play, these eventually became disconnected narratives, as the titles of subsequent productions reveal. Unfortunately the surviving plays of Sophocles and Euripides (except for a substantial fragment, discussed in a later chapter) are all apparently from separate productions, making it difficult to determine how they fit with the rest of their trilogies. And of course the same can be said of the surviving Aeschylean plays. The *Oresteia*, with its nuanced symbolism and thematic coherence, represents a pinnacle of achievement, and we can only speculate that the poet was able to bind *Laius*, *Oedipus*, and *Seven Against Thebes* with similar artistry.

All the plays in this trilogy and its satyr play would be performed with two actors, but as the following discussion will illustrate, the most emotional exchanges are between Eteocles (played by the protagonist), king of Thebes, and the chorus of young women. The second actor (deuteragonist) took on the role of the messenger, who delivers news of the invasion and its outcome.

Structure and Themes

Prologue

There was no curtain to be raised; the actor playing Eteocles simply enters from an *eisodos*, and the play is set in motion. He identifies himself and addresses an assembled group of Theban men, supernumeraries whose entrance may have preceded his. (Surviving scripts contain no stage directions, so performance details must be gleaned from the text.) The prologue, consisting of the first seventy-seven lines, wastes no time. The king exhorts these citizens to defend their home against an Argive attack predicted by an unnamed prophet. A scout now enters from the opposite *eisodos* with an eye-witness report of the seven enemy chieftains sacrificing a bull, pouring its blood into a black shield, and invoking gods of war and panic in an oath to take the city or die in the attempt. They have drawn lots for their positions at the seven gates of Thebes.

This ominous and highly charged account acknowledges the supernatural backdrop to the action of the play, an important consideration that pervades much of Greek tragedy. Beneath the material reality of the theater exists an unseen nexus of forces that includes past events, offstage characters, the will of gods, and malignant powers activated by language. Aeschylus, arguably more vividly than Sophocles or Euripides, articulates what Andrew Sofer, adapting the astrophysicist's concept of "dark matter," describes as "the invisible dimension of theater that escapes visual detection, even though its effects are felt everywhere in performance" (2013: 3). Sofer includes absent characters and narrations of past or off stage events (including messenger speeches in tragedy) in his analysis, but also the realm of hallucinations, ghosts, and demons. An understanding of this spectral dimension is crucial to analyzing the three tragedies discussed in this volume—and much of surviving tragedy—but it is particularly pertinent to *Seven*. In this seemingly static drama, at least in terms of stage action, events are set in motion by a curse, reinforced by an oath, in essence a conditional curse; both speech acts acknowledge a reality beyond an audience's perception but still within their understanding of how the universe operates.

Oaths and curses are part of the communication between the mortal world, existing in the tangible realm represented in the theater, and the superhuman world empowering those speech acts, a world that occupies a psychic space seldom visible but always potent. There is a reciprocal process by which the gods participate through oracles and portents: a Theban seer has interpreted the bird-signs sent from the gods that warn of the invasion. Even the lots drawn by the Argive leaders were divinely ordained according to ancient Greek beliefs. Eteocles participates in this system of communication with a prayer that concludes the prologue. He calls on Zeus, Earth, the protecting deities of the city, his father's curse, and the Erinys (Fury), the embodiment and fulfillment of that curse: do not let our city be enslaved; protect us so that we can continue to make offerings to you. The prologue concludes with his exit.

Parodos

The parados, or entrance song of the chorus as it arrives through one of the *eisodoi*, is a continuation of the emotional trajectory initiated in the foreboding prologue. A group of frightened girls, who self-identify as "a suppliant band of virgins" (110), runs into the orchestra; their first word, "I shriek" (78), establishes the mood. The song vividly signifies that the invaders are drawing closer: a cloud of dust swirls in the air; horse hooves resound in their ears, and thanks to the onomatopoeia, "*hoplokup' ōti*," in the audience's as well. In her study of the soundscapes of Aeschylean tragedy, Sarah Nooter (2017: 74–7) draws attention to the "predominately spatial and centripetal component" of the aural experience. The chorus describes the approach of the enemy using the emotional dochmiac meter, interspersed with phatic utterances (*iō, iō; e, e, e*), and disjointed prayers.[1]

The virgins embody the vulnerability of the city under attack. The symbolism would be evident to an Athenian audience because the center of their city, the Acropolis, housed the Parthenon, the temple of the virgin goddess Athena. But the orderly regularity of their own rituals, some conducted by virgins such as these, would be a sharp contrast to the agitated, chaotic prayers enacted before them.

First Episode

The first episode is dominated by Eteocles berating the terrified women for their inappropriate rituals. Acknowledgment of a choral song by a character is unusual, to be found more in early than later tragedy (Hutchinson 1985: 75). It occurs in Aeschylus' *Eumenides* when Apollo harangues the chorus of Furies after their entrance song; they too are active participants in the rest of the drama. Because *Seven* is a two-actor play the chorus has a greater role in the action and dialogue than later three-actor plays. We get a sense of tragedy in its formative stages when it was a call and response between a single actor and chorus. This episode is comprised of a speech or *rhesis* by Eteocles, and a response by the chorus in either lyrics or chants, a format known as an *epirrhematic dialogue*, and then finally a dialogue consisting of one-liners (*stichomythia*) in iambic trimeters (the conversational meter of tragedy) between Eteocles and the chorus leader, or *coryphaeus*, an anonymous, undifferentiated member of the chorus who spoke individually on its collective behalf.

Eteocles responds to the women's entrance with a misogynistic diatribe (182–202). He addresses them as "intolerable creatures" and wishes:

> May I never share my home with the tribe of women.
> When she is doing well her boldness is intolerable,
> but frightened she's even more a danger to home and state.

Exemplifying gender tensions inherent in Greek tragedy, his vituperative outburst is also in keeping with earlier Greek poets such as the seventh-century Semonides of Amorgos, who categorized women's faults in terms of animal equivalents. It has often been noted that tragedy sustains an implicit critique of women; the husband-murdering Clytemnestra in Aeschylus' *Agamemnon* and the chorus of vampiric Furies who hound her son Orestes for his matricide are perhaps the most extreme examples of the potential evils of women.[2] Four decades later Euripides makes Hippolytus, in his name-play, launch a similar invective against women-kind (again "the tribe of women"), although it would be incorrect to ascribe these sentiments to the playwrights themselves.

Nonetheless misogynistic invective is a commonplace, not to be underestimated in terms of how it represents contemporary Greek stereotypes, but also worth unpacking for how it reflects themes of the drama.

Eteocles objects to the chorus' presence outside the house and repeatedly exhorts them to return inside: "stay within and do no harm" (201). Their terror, he complains, is infecting the mood of the city. The opinion that women should know their place and not interfere in the affairs of men goes back as far as Homer's *Iliad* (6.490–92), when the Trojan Hector rebukes his wife Andromache for suggesting a defensive strategy: "go inside and weave," he tells her, "war is men's affair." The ideal is maintained throughout Greek thought. In his *Oeconomicus*, the fourth-century historian Xenophon ascribes similar sentiments to a self-satisfied Athenian gentleman who explains to his wife how the innate nature of men makes them more suited for outdoor work, while women are better suited, because of their inherent timidity, for domestic chores indoors. The principle manifests throughout tragedy: Sophocles' Electra, for example, comments on her own inappropriate appearance outside the house (*Electra* 119). Space is gendered in Greek tragedy, as it was in ancient Greek society. But all tragedy is set outside; there are no interior scenes. In later tragedy, a female character might stand outside a house, represented by the stage building, or *skene*, but that is not yet part of the architecture here.

The space that Aeschylus creates in his *Seven* is civic and public—a king addresses his male citizens and sends them off to battle—hardly an appropriate place for a group of young women, with one important exception. Women and girls played vital roles in the religious life of a city, and that is the motivation for this chorus. They have come to pray for the salvation of their city, but Eteocles finds their prayers and supplication disruptive and inappropriate. The scene emphasizes the power of the spoken word in a ritual context: the purpose of Eteocles' scathing admonishments is to stop the chorus from uttering ill-omened words that could provoke divine displeasure. It is a concern that aligns with the supernatural effect of his father's curse, the root cause of his present crisis, and thus furnishes an outstanding example of the damaging potential of ritual language improperly used.

The exchange between the chorus and Eteocles serves two important dramatic functions. In the most effective and immediate way possible, and deploying the social conventions of his time, Aeschylus establishes a mood of fear and distress with the panicked entrance of the chorus and its interaction with Eteocles. The action begins at a critical moment when consequences of the two earlier tragedies coalesce; the trilogy culminates in the actualization of the curse that will bring down the family once and for all. The chorus helps to heighten the atmosphere of terror and chaos that this curse manifests. This mood could be powerfully enhanced by background noises: clashing metal, heavy thuds, produced by what Pollux describes as a "thunder machine," perhaps a drum and cymbals. Then again, the chorus gets the point across very vividly by echoing the tumult of the siege outside the walls; they bring the exterior invisible space into the city with descriptions of what they hear. At the same time the chorus also articulates an interior, psychological space by embodying the extreme fear of Eteocles. His efforts to control the agitated young women seem to externalize a desperate need to check his own panic.

The early moments of the play feature a concentrated series of ritual events connected in some way to the curse of Oedipus. The present conflict between the brothers is the result of that curse. On the surface, this first episode is a simplistic form of drama performed by the protagonist and the chorus or *coryphaeus*, yet the text pulsates with energy, emotion, and danger. Aeschylus deploys the elements of his art to their maximum potential. He had a particular talent for representing fear in a visceral and powerful manner, as Jaqueline de Romilly observed in her book on the topic (1958), and the text thus far illustrates.

First Stasimon

Eteocles departs and the chorus performs its first stasimon, literally "standing song," marking the end of the first episode. Having taken its station in the orchestra, it is by no means standing still. From the text it is difficult to tell exactly what Eteocles' remonstrations accomplished, but it is a good assumption that the women's movements have become less disorganized as they approach the gods' statues to make their prayers. The second half of the ode, however, is a vivid narrative of the rape and pillage in store for a conquered city. These tropes derive from accounts of the sack of Troy, a theme in Greek narrative poetry and Athenian public art (Hutchinson 1985: 89–90). And the plight of women in war informs some of Euripides' most moving choral odes, including those of the *Trojan Women*, *Hecuba*, and *Iphigenia at Aulis*, produced at the end of the century.

As the ode concludes, the chorus observes the entrances of Eteocles and then the messenger. In the absence of stage directions, we rely on the chorus and characters to announce an entrance, a fundamental axiom of tragic stagecraft identified by Oliver Taplin (1977), although contested or modified by other scholars.

Second Episode

In the second episode (369–652) a messenger describes the shield of each of the seven enemy chieftains: the blazons on these shields symbolize the character and aspirations of their owners. From our perspective the episode, with its balanced structure and catalogue-like features, seems unnaturally formal, but similar devices in epic and archaic poetry (composed in the seventh and sixth centuries BCE) testify to its appeal for a fifth-century audience, who still attended public recitals of Homeric poetry. The catalogue tradition goes back as far as the second book of the *Iliad* dedicated to a list of the Greek ships. Helen's identification of the Greek heroes, as she stands on the walls of Troy, could be the inspiration for this catalogue of shields (Hutchinson 1985: 105). Evidently ancient audiences enjoyed the list or catalogue format, since it shows up in other genres and other tragedies.

The influence of earlier poetic structures and themes is evident. Most of *Iliad* 18 is a detailed description of the shield of Achilles, replete with animated scenes of war and peace. A separate poem, *Aspis* ("The Shield"), attributed to the seventh-century epic poet Hesiod (although most scholars doubt this authorship) is an extensive description of the shield of Heracles. The fascination carried over into the visual arts. Numerous vase paintings from the sixth and fifth centuries feature warriors and heroes with elaborately embellished shields. Be that as it may, the shields described by the messenger are probably not based on real objects, but have a deeper symbolic resonance. The prevalence of narrative as opposed to dramatic action is typical of early tragedy (Hutchinson 1985: 103). Realism is not the object here. Rather than staging a conversational dialogue, Aeschylus sets up a balanced series of speeches (collectively known as the *Redepaare*): each section consists of the messenger's account (15–25 lines) of one of the enemy warriors and his shield matched by Eteocles' response (of equal length), which assigns a corresponding Theban warrior at the appropriate city gate. A short choral song concludes each set of paired speeches. The scene, despite its rigid formality, contributes much to the themes of the play and the characterization of Eteocles.

The messenger's account emphasizes the Argive hubris, blasphemy, and boastfulness. Eteocles counters by highlighting the justice, reverence, and courage of his warriors. For example, the first Argive, Tydeus, rails against the prophet Amphiaraus' warning not to cross the river Ismenus into Theban territory; the "sign" (*sēma*, 387) on his shield is a full moon and stars. Eteocles interprets this "nighttime" shield emblem as a portent of its owner's impending death and assigns the

Theban Melanippus to stand against him under the auspices of *Dikē* (Justice) at the Proitan gate. The chorus emphasizes that Melanippus will go forth "justly" on behalf of the city (417–21). The messenger then reports that the gigantic Argive Capaneus drew the lot for the Electran gates. His blasphemous boast, "inappropriate for a mortal" (425), is that he will destroy the city, whether the gods are willing or not, and that not even Zeus, whose thunderbolts he likens to a noonday sun, can prevent him. The sign on his shield is a "naked, fire-bearing man" whose words, "I will burn the city" (434–5), are written in golden letters. Eteocles identifies the speech of Capaneus as irreverent and predicts his destruction by fire. His emphasis on *dusphema*, careless irreligious language, is consistent with his attempt to control the ritual language of the chorus. He assigns the warrior Polyphontes, a man "of fiery spirit," to fight against him with the support of the gods. The chorus contextualizes the vaunts of Capaneus in terms of their own concerns and prays that he be smitten by lightening before he bursts into their virginal chambers.

This symmetrical pattern continues up to the final set of speeches (631–85) in which the messenger reveals that the seventh gate is assigned to Polyneices, Eteocles' brother. He describes his shield (642–8):

> … a perfect circle, newly made,
> a double symbol artfully fixed upon it:
> a woman, going first, modestly leads
> a man armed, it seems, in hammered gold.
> Justice (*Dikē*), she claims to be, and her words
> are written out: "I will bring this man back,
> and he will possess the city, and walk throughout
> his ancestral home."

Five of the six preceding shield emblems—only that of the reverent prophet Amphiaraus has no decoration—signify the arrogance and unruly speech of the invaders, whom Eteocles matches against his own righteous warriors (reverently silent, if they are represented by mute actors), but this final blazon disturbs that balance of opposites. Polyneices is invading his own city; he seeks his own *Dikē*. Aeschylus does not specify that Polyneices had a claim to justice because his brother refused to give up the throne, although that seems a logical inference. Leading up to this, the assignment of Theban warriors counterbalanced the Argive champions, but the account of Polyneices' shield emblem, highlighting *Dikē*, "Justice," now reveals a sameness rather than a difference between the two brothers. Far from being a formulaic moment of superficial pageantry, the balanced structure of the scene lays bare the overlap between self and other. As each other's double, and eventually each other's killer, the brothers destabilize notions of enmity and justice.

Eteocles' work has been to read the enemy shields and then overwrite their symbols with his response. This has been intensely scrutinized by Froma Zeitlin in an ground-breaking study, which she describes as "an experiment in the decoding of an ancient text in the light of the findings and methods of modern semiotic theory" (1982: 9). Zeitlin concludes that Eteocles' interpretation of the Argive shields inevitably leads him to his brother at the seventh gate. Here is what she has to say about Polyneices' shield and Eteocles' decision to fight against him:

> The war throughout [the *Redepaare*] has been a war of words, with the aim of appropriating the enemy's language so as to claim their words for Thebes. But these actions also repeated the act of appropriation by which Eteokles claimed hegemony of Thebes for himself and expelled his brother from the city and from his father's house.
>
> (1982: 137)

As Zeitlin goes on to suggest, Eteocles' theft of the throne is matched by "a semantic theft, a stealing of words. Polyneikes by the device on his shield and the message, which it bears, has now appropriated the *Dikē*, which Eteokles had kept for himself." This sophisticated analysis probes the semantic intricacy of Aeschylus' text in order to correlate the merging of the brothers' identity with their incestuous origins—the union of their father with his and their shared mother.

Tragic Decision-Making

While bringing these tensions into focus, the shield scene moves the plot forward with Eteocles' fatal decision. Self-aware and resolute he epitomizes Aeschylean notions of individual responsibility in the context of larger external forces, "dark matter," as it were. The tragic hero's downfall is a combination of preordained forces, notably his father's curse, and his own personal choice. It is a uniquely tragic motivation, neither entirely a matter of free will nor entirely deterministic. The overlap is alien to our sensibilities, a product of centuries of ethical humanism that distinguishes between the two. But the audience of tragedy, schooled in the tradition of Homeric heroes whose individual decisions are made against the backdrop of divine power, could recognize an over-determined universe in which tragic characters' choices mirror greater cosmic designs.

After Eteocles elects to fight against his brother, the chorus leader responds. Instead of a short lyric (in the dochmiac meter) by the chorus, as in the six previous groupings, the six lines (677–82), spoken in iambic trimeters (the "conversational" meter of tragedy), disrupt the pattern with a warning to Eteocles not to "be like in temperament" to his brother. A *coryphaeus* seldom speaks more than four lines, so this longer utterance underscores the dreadful decision to spill fraternal blood, which complicates Eteocles' commitment to protecting his city. The *coryphaeus* immediately situates fratricide in a religious context: bloodshed in battle can be ritually expiated, but no purification is possible for killing one's own family. Nonetheless Eteocles does not waver from his decision; its gravity and his own responsibility are emphasized by the subsequent exchange with the chorus, whose brief strophe (stanza), returning to dochmiacs, the predominant meter of the parodos, heightens the emotional intensity.

The pattern repeats four times with the chorus beseeching Eteocles to restrain his anger and hold back from combat and Eteocles insistently referring to his father's curse as an inexorable force. The episode ends with four sets of stichomythia (712–20), a single line of iambic trimeter exchanged between speakers (here Eteocles answers the *coryphaeus*), a common element of tragic dialogue, particularly in a heated argument. As Derek Collins (2004: 28–9) suggests, the device functions as "a formalized poetic adaptation of a 'live' mode of contestation." The Athenians were notoriously fond of legal and political debates, which tragedy reflects with a focus on debates and rhetoric, as we shall observe in the next chapters. Moreover, the argumentative tone of the exchange accentuates Eteocles' responsibility for his decision—emphasizing the possibility that he could change his mind—while simultaneously acknowledging the malignant force of the curse that pushes him toward that decision.

Tragic plots often involve characters making difficult choices that shape the action of the drama but are informed by past events. Such decisions inevitably reflect the personality and ethics of that character yet also involve forces beyond their control. A classic example is the dilemma that Aeschylus' Agamemnon faces at Aulis, recounted by the chorus in the parodos: should he immolate his lovely young daughter, Iphigenia, the "treasure of my household," to get favorable winds to send his armada to Troy? He is in a terrible bind because Zeus demands that he retrieve Helen from the Trojans. With lapidary finesse the poet represents the cognitive process of his character through the voice of the chorus, which describes the girl's saffron robes pouring to the ground. A symbolic stage action revisits his decision later in the play when he returns home to Clytemnestra: the victorious king must decide whether to walk on the precious tapestries that his wife spreads before his feet. He does indeed choose to destroy the "wealth of his house," as he unknowingly walks to his death. Aeschylus complicates Agamemnon's moral agency, however, by reminding us of the curse on the house of Atreus, launched by Thyestes against his brother Atreus.[3] The agency of Agamemnon is thus enmeshed in an inherited curse, and he is forced to make his difficult choice, one might surmise, because of that curse. This phenomenon of double determinism, an alignment of human choice and supernatural force, frames the decision of Eteocles, as we have seen.

Eteocles is both target and agent of his father's curse; like Agamemnon he moves of his own volition toward the fulfillment of that familial curse, but unlike Agamemnon he is apparently fully aware of its influence. The climax of the drama comes at the end of the *Redepaare* when he decides to meet his brother in mortal combat. Everything up to this point has emphasized the perilous state of affairs: the first messenger's description of the enemy at the gates, the terrified prayers of the chorus, and the messenger's accounts of the threatening blazons on the attackers' shields. When he learns of his brother's shield, he makes a grim conclusion that illustrates his comprehension of his difficult situation:

> O most miserable, god-maddened family of Oedipus,
> greatly hated by the gods. Alas, now indeed are
> my father's curses fulfilled. (653–5)

With this acknowledgment, it becomes obvious that the scene of precise, formal correspondences—all the more notable after the intense emotion and chaos of the chorus in the parodos, first episode, and first stasimon—reflects a spectral background of malevolent efficiency as the curse locks its grip on the two brothers.

Second Stasimon

Structurally the shield scene is at the mid-point of the play, balanced in chiastic formation (a-b-c-b-a) with a choral ode and epirrhematic dialogue (see above) on either side. The symmetry emphasizes the inevitability of its consequences. After demanding his armor, Eteocles departs to meet his brother; it is his final exit. The chorus, full of foreboding dread, sings the second stasimon: its first word *pephrika* (720), "I shudder," sets the tone as it contemplates the history of the family curse embodied as an Erinys, "a goddess not like the gods, an evil prophet in every way" (721–3), now moving with inexorable precision toward its targets at the seventh gate.

Simon Goldhill (1996: 50) describes tragic choral songs as a "hinge" between scenes and characters, "always looking back to the scene just past, or forward to the action to come." This ode does indeed look in both directions. Whereas both preceding choral songs responded to the immediate crisis, the second stasimon reflects on the fateful decision of Eteocles by surveying past events in his unfortunate family, and forecasting the inevitable fratricide, to be reported in the short third episode. The first part of the ode is a recapitulation of the two preceding tragedies. From it we learn that Laius, father of Oedipus and subject of the first play, went against Apollo's oracle, which forbade him to reproduce, and that Oedipus bedded his own mother. According to this version it was when Oedipus learned the truth of his identity that he blinded himself (as he does in Sophocles' version), and cursed his sons, the product of his repellent incest (which does not happen in Sophocles' *Oedipus Tyrannus*).

Typically a single tragedy will compress its action into a critical few hours; from the audience's perspective it occurs in something approximating "real time." But inevitably the past intrudes on the present, as it does here. Tragic temporality expands by various devices including narrations of the history behind the action and occasionally also its future. When the chorus sings the second stasimon, it becomes a depersonalized voice with access to a deep well of cultural memory. Eteocles has made his fateful choice thereby fulfilling not only his father's curse, as he acknowledges, but also the dire warning of Apollo's oracle before Oedipus was conceived. Past, present, and future are interwoven in way that reflects the performative power of ritual language, most palpably represented in the chilling description of the invaders' oath, Eteocles' concern with appropriate prayers, his vow to the gods, and the emphasis on the blasphemous vaunts of the invaders in the preceding episode. Thus elements of the early part of the play are enfolded within a reciprocal system of communication that fuses mortal and immortal spheres and encompasses all three generations of the family.

When it sings this expansive narrative the chorus seems to step out of its persona as a group of frightened young girls to become an authoritative voice of history. A tragic chorus has an innate authority derived in part from the important ritual function of choruses in other contexts, but the dramatic persona of a chorus is not necessarily associated with authoritative utterances: household slaves in Aeschylus' *Libation Bearers*, ordinary local women in Sophocles' *Women of Trachis*, or Euripides' *Medea*, for example, all articulate an understanding of events in a larger context. How does a chorus' dramatic identity, especially one of humble status, jibe with its role as omniscient commentator on the action? If the choral persona is that of Argive or Theban elders (as they are in Aeschylus' *Agamemnon*, Sophocles' *Oedipus* and *Antigone*) their gender and age might imbue them with the requisite authority to interpret events. Even so the chorus might display its all too human limitations. "I have the power to tell," (104) proclaims the chorus of *Agamemnon* before it recounts the sacrifice of Iphigenia at Aulis. Yet despite this claim, it is often befuddled or reluctant to accept the inevitable conclusion that its king has committed appalling crimes and that his wife Clytemnestra is going to murder him when he returns home from Troy. Even though the elders sing about the dangers of excessive wealth and the lurking presence of the vengeful Erinyes they seem unable to apply this knowledge to Agamemnon (Fletcher 1999, 2014).

The character of the chorus of *Seven* seems disconnected from its function as an authoritative voice in a very different way. In the first part of the play the collective personality of the chorus is that of a group of distressed virgins. Indeed, their characterization is consistent with ancient Greek stereotypes of young women (Fletcher 2007). The virgin or *parthenos* was a socially constructed identity: references to young women on the cusp of adulthood frequently emphasize their flightiness, hysteria, and disruptive behavior. The unruly chorus of Aeschylus' *Suppliant Women* exemplifies this paradigm. The Theban virgins whom Eteocles castigates are, of course, terrified of the enemy invasion, a fear that shapes their initial emotional state, but they also conform to this stereotype. On the other hand, they are, by the shield scene, although still concerned with their own safety, much more rational. The *coryphaeus* urges caution and self-control as Eteocles makes his fateful decision to meet his brother at the seventh gate and even refers to him as *teknon*, "child" (686). The chorus' new sober wisdom seems so different from its earlier behavior that one scholar argued that the *choreutae* had changed masks to indicate their new persona (Solmsen 1937), an unlikely and singular example of tragic dramaturgy.

A better way to think about the chorus is to understand that it may oscillate between a specific dramatic identity and its function as a detached "voice of the poet." As Goldhill (1996: 254–5) observes:

> It is, in short, the tension between authoritative, ritual, mythic utterance and specific, marginal, partial utterance that gives the chorus its special voice in tragedy … The chorus requires the audience to engage in a constant renegotiation of where the authoritative voice lies. It sets in play an authoritative collective voice, but surrounds it with other dissenting voices. The chorus allows a wider picture of the action to develop and also remains one of the many views expressed. The chorus thus is a key dramatic device for setting commentary, reflection, and authoritative voice in play as part of tragic conflict.

The second stasimon ends by recounting the curse of Oedipus that his sons "divide his possessions between them with iron-wielding hands," a malediction to be accomplished by the Erinys, who occupies a significant position as the last word of the ode; her mention also returns to the thoughts of the first lines.

Third Episode

With these words still in the air, the messenger arrives. The third episode is short, less than thirty lines, wedged between the choral odes. Although messenger speeches tend to be considerably longer, this brief account of the inevitable death of the two brothers typifies how tragedy eschews the depiction of violence in the theater. Addressing them as "children, nurslings of your mothers," a reminder of their youth and vulnerability, he announces that the maidens have nothing to fear; the city has averted disaster. In a survey of choral identities, Helene Foley (2003) makes the generic observation that choruses are survivors, as this one surely is. It now begins a long lament with a short passage of anapests, a recitative meter, before starting their song (833–1004).

Exodus

The chorus dominates in the remainder of the tragedy (1005–78) with a lamentation for the catastrophic deaths of the city's ruling family. At this point we must take into account serious questions about the authenticity of portions of the exodus. Our text, transmitted in the form of several medieval manuscripts supplemented by a few scraps of papyrus, contains several suspicious passages. Most scholars are inclined to view these as interpolations, additions inserted into Aeschylus' script perhaps in a revision during the late fifth or early fourth century BCE. The content and specific phrases bear similarities to Sophocles' *Antigone* and Euripides' *Phoenician Women*; some of the vocabulary choices and syntax seem more in line with later Attic dialect and are distinctly un-Aeschylean; there are awkward sections and transitions that suggest a tampering with the original text. At lines 861–74 the chorus breaks off from its song and in chanting anapests apparently greets Antigone and Ismene, the two daughters of Oedipus, who join in the dirge. While the sisters' presence as mourners might seem natural, their appearance at this point is clumsy, unmotivated, and ignored for an awkward length of time. Furthermore the anapestic chant disrupts the symmetry of the choral lyrics. The text attributes some of the lyrics to Ismene and Antigone, although these verses could have originally belonged to the chorus. It seems most likely that the original text ends at line 1004 or that a few lines were excised to accommodate the revision. The text as we have it indicates the sisters' presence at 1005–1053, when a herald comes to announce decrees authorizing the burial of Eteocles with full honors and forbidding the burial of Polyneices, whose corpse is to be left for the dogs and crows. Antigone responds that she intends to defy the decree despite the herald's warnings. The chorus splits into two groups: one vows to accompany Antigone and the other to help Ismene bury Eteocles. There has been no preparation in the play thus far for this event.

Arguments against the authenticity of these passages are convincing (e.g., Thalmann 1978: 137–41; Hutchinson 1985: 209–11; Sommerstein 2010: 90–3). To introduce an extraneous complication at the conclusion of the play (let alone the entire trilogy), focused so intensely on the curse of Oedipus and its destruction of the family line, seems pointless. At several points, the text has suggested that Eteocles' self-sacrifice will both fulfill and end the curse (e.g., 699–701), and there is no indication of further blight against the family or the city. The influence of Sophocles' *Antigone* (probably the first version of the defiant princess's burial of Polyneices) is obvious. If *Seven* was restaged in the late fifth century as a stand-alone play, it is possible that the producer added this material as a segue into what had then become a famous conclusion to the Theban saga. But while it would be appropriate for a trilogy that had explored the dimensions of intergenerational strife and the interlocking force of oracles and curses to conclude with the extirpation of a family, an ending that anticipates further disruption seems anticlimactic. As William Thalmann (1978: 141) puts it, if the ending of the play is genuine, it suggests that "the family survives in attenuated form, and the play trails off indecisively." And then there is the matter of Aeschylus' artistic sensibilities: the elegant structure of the tragedy, with the central shield scene balanced on either side by corresponding scenes and songs, is marred by the unsatisfying ending. Furthermore, the simultaneous presence of three speaking actors, playing the roles of the herald, Antigone, and Ismene, violates the production conventions of the time. In the final analysis, arguments against the authenticity of the ending are too compelling to ignore, although in all likelihood very little, if anything at all, has been removed to accommodate the revised exodus.

The controversy about the ending of Aeschylus' *Seven* exemplifies the tenuous state of knowledge about much of tragedy. Any assumptions about how a trilogy could end are based on limited evidence. Similarly, attempts to reconstruct the performance of tragedy have to glean the text and material culture for details. With these considerable limitations in mind, we turn now to the first production of Aeschylus' *Seven* in the theater of Dionysus.

Production

For the historian of the genre attempting to reconstruct the earliest staging of tragedy, evidence for ancient productions is frustratingly sparse. In his list of the six elements of tragedy, Aristotle puts *opsis* ("spectacle") last. But although he provides very little information about the visual components of theater, he recognizes the importance of *schemata*, which probably included "figures of movement on the stage, including blocking (working out the movement and positioning of actors), gestures, and even dancing," as G. M. Sifakis (2013: 60) argues. Aeschylus, according to the *Suda*, established a reputation for impressive spectacles, not only with choral performance, but also costumes, "altars and tombs, trumpets, apparitions, and Erinyes," and he was responsible for adding color to tragic masks, making them appear more alive (discussed in Pickard-Cambridge 1968: 190; Wiles 2007: 20). Even though we lack material evidence to substantiate these accounts, the texts of Aeschylus supply tantalizing hints of his theatricality, the most famous being the magnificent tapestry scene of the *Agamemnon*.

But there is much that the surviving texts do not reveal. Without stage directions, scholars must extrapolate details of actors' and choruses' movements, entrances and exits, the presence of mute actors, and props from the scripts. Mapping these speculative reconstructions onto the physical remains of the theater, whose architecture is lost in the dust of time, poses a unique set of challenges. The theater of Dionysus in its current state—a curved orchestra of stone tiles surrounded by a semicircle of tiers of stone benches—did not exist when *Seven* was originally produced. The audience sat in stadium-style wooden benches. The shape of the orchestra, as we have already noted, may have been curved or rectilinear, but in either case it was probably simply hardened earth. The *skene* building, such a prominent feature in subsequent tragedy, serves no purpose in early tragedy. One of the most conspicuous features of the genre before 458 BCE (the production of the *Oresteia*) is the apparent lack of any sort of backdrop, and that is certainly the case with *Seven*.

In his influential study, *The Stagecraft of Aeschylus* (1977), Taplin catalogues and scrutinizes references to actors' entrances and exits in the texts of the playwright's seven surviving tragedies. The basic premise is that "all significant visual aspects of stage management are singled out for attention in the words" (1977: 75). While scholars have nearly universally accepted Aristotle's division of tragedy (prologue, parodos, episode, stasimon, etc.), Taplin contends that a more useful way of defining the structural elements of tragedy is by considering the entrances and exits of actors, which divide a play into "acts." This much we can deduce: characters and chorus made their entrances and exits through one of the two *eisodoi*. Eteocles would arrive from the same *eisodos* as the chorus, in other words through the corridor that signified the city, but he would have made his final exit through the opposite *eisodos*, through which the messenger came and left, taking him to the border of the city.

By a careful analysis of surviving texts of Aeschylean drama, supplemented by a conservative use of later comments such as those of Aristotle and Pollux, and a cautious examination of the remains of the theater of Dionysus in Athens we can imagine, albeit speculatively, the experience of *Seven*'s original audience. It is important to remember that although the tetralogy or simply one of its plays would be reproduced in other theaters throughout the ancient Mediterranean world, Aeschylus composed it for a specific venue and time: the annual festival of Dionysus in the god's sacred precinct, which included its rough-hewn theater. So what did spectators see as they sat on those (hopefully cushioned) wooden benches on a chilly day in March 467 BCE? We begin with the chorus, the heart of tragedy for an ancient audience.

Song and Dance

Omnipresent and positioned between the acting space and the audience, the chorus members are a link between the tragic action and its spectators. *Choreia* signifies the song and dance of the chorus, ephemeral ingredients of tragedy that guided and enhanced the audience's experience. All choral songs included dance moves, and the chorus responded to events in the drama with gestures (*cheironomia*) and poses (*schemata*), some of which the chorus describes. In the parodos it implores the gods to heed its prayers "made with outstretched hands" (179). Earlier it wonders: "Should I fall at the feet of the statues of the gods?" (94–5) All indications are that it moves, either collectively or in groups of two or three, toward cult statues set in the orchestra. After news of the mutual fratricide, the chorus compares the movement of their hands to oars (854–60) in the second stasimon. This signifier of lamentation is represented on vase paintings dating back to the Dark Ages; the Dipylon Vase (*c.* 750 BCE), an Athenian grave marker, shows mourners performing precisely this gesture.

Ancient commentators indicate that between its odes as well the chorus used movements to interpret the action and speech of characters. It would be a mistake to imagine the group standing still and silent when they are not singing or engaging with the characters. A vital presence throughout the drama, the chorus could intensify the mood and was an integral component of the visual impact of the production even when it was silent.

Materialities of Production: Masks, Costumes, and Props

Actors are the nexus of meaning in drama. As McAuley (2000: 90) observes:

> It is through the body and person of the actor that all the contributing systems of meaning (visual, vocal, spatial, fictional) are activated, and the actor/performer is without doubt the most important agent in all the signifying processes involved in the performance event.

The actors of tragedy enhanced their contributions to this signifying system by means of masks, costumes, props, and gestures. In addition, the performer's body becomes meaningful in its relationship to other people, an ephemeral variable, but one for which our text offers some guidance. Writing specifically about the actor in ancient Greek theater, Kostas Valakas (2002: 77) sums up the vectors that converge on that body:

> [I]ts positions and displacements within the theatrical space; its orientation and relation to the public, to other actors and to theatrical objects; the direction of the axis of the body; the positions of the limbs and the distribution of weight; the visible and audible expressions of the body, mainly movements and gestures, speech and song.

Seven is full of people, although only two have speaking roles, whose energies combine, collide, and counterpoint each other. As previously noted, the *protagonist*, or "first contender," played Eteocles, and the second actor, or *deuteragonist*, took the role of the messenger. Not only is *Seven* a two-actor play, but it has only two roles for them to play. Compare *Persians* in which two actors divided the roles of Xerxes, the Queen, a messenger, and the ghost of Darius between them, role changes made possible by masks and costumes.

Masks, with all their transformative potential, characterize ancient Greek drama and emphasize its fictionality and otherness. A few fifth-century ceramic vessels, including the Pronomos Vase, depict actors with their masks, often with strings or straps showing; they are life-size or slightly larger, constructed from stuccoed linen to which hair and beards are attached. As Sommerstein (2010: 41) observes, they are more like "head coverings." C. W. Marshall (1999) emphasizes their generic qualities: gender, age, and status are conveyed, but not individual personalities. *Seven*'s chorus of young virgins, for instance, would have pale skin (a convention for depicting women also found on vase paintings). When a mask, devoid of specificity, is animated by performer, it exerts a reciprocal effect on that actor, as David Wiles (2007) has argued, turning him

Figure 5 *The Phiale Painter. Two-handled jar (pelike) with actors preparing for a performance. Greek, Athens, c. 430 BCE. Courtesy Boston Museum of Fine Arts*

into the character that he represents. Spectators, in turn, project emotions and character, derived from the text embodied by the actor, on the blank canvas of the generic mask. The relationship between mask and spectator is tightened if, as Peter Meineck (2014) argues, the physical contours of the mask required the actor to speak directly to the audience, rather than to other characters. The closest audience members would be no less than ten meters away—many were much further. There was nothing in the mask's construction to enhance the acoustics of the actor's voice. Acting was consequently more a form of declamation to the spectators than a two-way conversation between characters, a feature that seems more pronounced in the early tragedies.

In other respects, the representation of the body in tragedy is highly stylized. Costumes enhanced the actors' physical presence. Vase paintings of actors (identifiable by their masks) indicate that tragic costumes distinguished characters from everyday people. A ceramic vessel from mid-fifth-century Athens depicts two actors, as the mask on the floor between them confirms, in the process of dressing for their roles (Figure 5). One performer is pulling on a calf-high boot with pointed toe and flat sole, common footwear for tragic actors. In her study of evidence for tragic garb, Rosie Wyles (2011) discerns an evolution in costume conventions over the fifth century. Aeschylus, so says the *Suda*, introduced the sleeved robes that became conventional but were not worn in everyday life. Because these required sartorial skill, Wyles postulates a group of professional weavers and costume makers who created the bespoke wardrobes of individual productions. An ornately decorated, long-sleeved robe, as worn by the actor depicted on the Pronomos vase, would emphasize the exalted status of a king, although if Eteocles armed himself in the Shield Scene he would more likely be wearing a corselet. And indeed Wyles (2011: 23–4) finds evidence of bronze corselets used in tragedy. Nonetheless there are limitations to what we can say with certainty about costumes. We have already noted the phenomenon in Greek vase paintings of actors' masks "melting" into their faces and bodies, becoming part of the actor, as it were. As David Wiles (2007: 15) puts it: "We never see actors acting."

In addition to the two actors in the prologue there would be non-speaking extras, also masked and costumed, whom Eteocles addresses. Although it has been argued that Aeschylus expected his audience to imagine such a crowd (see Taplin 1977: 129–34), his reputation for creating spectacle suggests that the playwright might not pass up an opportunity for the dramatic effects of an assembly. Toward the end of his first speech Eteocles orders those citizens to rush out to defend the city against the impending attack of the Argives; at this point the notional group departs, leaving by the opposite *eisodos* through which they entered. Crowd scenes were (and still are) effective ways of creating powerful dramatic impressions, and Aeschylus is far from unique in their deployment. We shall see another example at the beginning of Sophocles' *Oedipus*, discussed in the next chapter.

The Shield Scene offers several opportunities for vivid dramaturgy deriving from mute extras, although there is no consensus on whether an original production used them. We are in the realm of informed speculation here, and the following discussion considers only what is possible given available data for the conventions of early drama. Arguing from a philological position, many scholars maintain that Aeschylus did not intend to have any mute supernumeraries present while Eteocles assigned Theban warriors to the city gates to meet their attackers. The strongest support for this contention is the different tenses in Eteocles' speeches, some past, others future, which suggest that certain heroes were already assigned to their gates, while others are chosen only as Eteocles speaks. But a more performance-oriented analysis speculates about what was possible in the context of early dramatic conventions. Of course, as argued above, ancient audiences were accustomed to the catalogue format, which allowed them to imagine each warrior and his shield; our notion of what made for good theater is not necessarily the same as that of ancient audiences'. Nonetheless, a fine translation (1973) by American poet, Anthony Hecht, in collaboration with classicist Helen Bacon, envisions a non-speaking actor stepping forward as Eteocles assigns a gate to each of the six Theban defenders. Aaron Poochigian (2007) suggests that these six warriors were already in the performance space, having entered with Eteocles, a group of silent attendants who take on the role of the six defenders when the time comes. According to the convention of two speaking actors, they cannot speak, but Aeschylus makes a virtue of necessity by letting their silence signify their compliance with Eteocles' anxiety about ill-omened speech.

The text gives some indication that Eteocles would start to arm himself in front of the audience as he prepared for the fratricidal combat at the seventh gate: he calls out for his greaves (676, leg armor), but needs say no more.[4] An ancient audience, familiar with the arming scenes of Homeric heroes (e.g., *Iliad* 3. 330–38, the arming of Paris) knew that a warrior put on his greaves first, followed by a corselet (which Eteocles could be wearing when he entered); then he buckles on his sword or spear and shield and finally dons his helmet. They had only to hear of the first item to know what happened next. The exchange between Eteocles and the chorus continues long enough for him to be armed by attendants who could have entered with each piece of armor. The effect would be quite stunning: the ill-starred protagonist, having made a decision that fulfills his father's curse, is then locked into his destiny as he fastens on each item. The pieces of armor function as a prop, defined by Sofer (2003) as "an inanimate object that is visibly manipulated by an actor in the course of performance," but whose "impact is mediated both by the gestures of the individual actor who handles the object" and the reception of the audience who understand that object to be a sign. And returning to Sofer's analysis of the "dark matter" of theater, we sense how Eteocles' armor is freighted with an occult power giving a dangerous materiality to the curse of Oedipus that drives his sons to kill each other.

The size of the theater, capable of holding thousands of spectators, not only precluded the small gestures and subtle nuances deployed by skilled actors in the smaller venues of modern times; it also hindered the effect of any small props, although there are several indications in the text of *Seven* of significant objects. When the chorus arrives, it refers to robes that the girls will offer to the gods. This form of devotion is well attested in other sources going back as far as Homer, and it was an important ritual in Athenian state religion. Arguably the most visible stage property would be the statues of the gods, to which the chorus refers as it enters, asking "which gods" to supplicate, and naming eight in their prayer. Later it explicitly refers to "this assembly of gods" (219–20), and Eteocles (264–6) asks them to move away from the statues. Ley (2007: 21) suggests that when they sing the first stasimon they move from the statues to "the open ground of the orchestra." Statues of the gods are "significant stage properties" and "constant presences throughout, casting a watchful eye over the action." Wiles (1993) suggests that if they were arranged in a semicircle around the orchestra, they would have formed seven spaces that reflected the seven gates of the city.

In the final moments of the play, the chorus is the focus in a crescendo of lamentation. Although persuasive arguments militate against the presence of Antigone and Ismene in the exodus, this does not rule out a tableau of the corpse of one or both of their brothers brought into the acting space by non-speaking extras to be mourned by their citizens and gazed upon by the audience. While tragedy avoids the depiction of violence in the material world of the theater—preferring instead accounts by messengers of gruesome offstage events, often in gory detail—the genre nonetheless has a notable predilection for its aftermath. Spectacles of wounded, suffering, or mutilated bodies, especially male bodies, are common throughout the corpus. Clytemnestra triumphantly displays the corpses of her husband, Agamemnon, and his captive, Cassandra. In Euripides' *Bacchae*, one of the last extant dramas (*c.* 405 BCE), the body parts of Pentheus, violently dismembered by his frenzied mother and a band of maenads, are pitifully reassembled before the audience. In *Seven*, a bier with the bloodied body of Eteocles, and possibly another with that of Polyneices, would be a natural and conventional way of letting the audience bear witness to the catastrophic fulfillment of the curse.

Satyr Drama

In any event, the acting space would be cleared after the departure of the chorus and given over to the final installment of the drama. Fragments of the satyr play, *Sphinx*, yield few clues about Aeschylus' treatment of the female monster that Oedipus vanquished, but a shard of pottery from a vase probably created shortly after the production shows a Sphinx gazing down on a group of seated satyrs wearing the costumes of elders and identifiable by their pointed ears, balding pates, and snub noses (discussed in Hutchinson 1985: xxi). Only one complete satyr drama survives, Euripides' *Cyclops*, but there is no consensus on what tetralogy it belonged to or its exact date. It adapts an episode from Homer's *Odyssey*, the encounter with Polyphemus, the one-eyed monstrous son of Poseidon. After the Cyclops devours several of the hero's men, Odysseus lets him drink his fill from his magic flask of wine and then blinds the drunken monster. The story lends itself perfectly to satyr drama because these hybrid creatures (half horse/half man) are often depicted in the retinue of Dionysus or in some form of drunken revelry. In Euripides' adaptation they have been trapped on the Cyclops' island, devoid of wine, and eagerly assist in the operation to defeat him.

   Although satyr choruses were conspicuous with their erect *phalloi* (visible in the Pronomos vase), and behaved with comical lewdness, satyr drama has its serious side. An ancient scholar described the genre as "tragedy at play." To be sure, Euripides' *Cyclops* displays the consequences of Polyphemus' blasphemy—the monster declares that he is superior to Zeus at one point—ideas that we find throughout tragedy. Considering the genre in its social context, Edith Hall (1998) has theorized that satyr drama, by representing "ithyphallic men behaving badly," served to restore the masculine ego threatened by the "feminine" emotions of pity and fear elicited by the preceding tragedies. In a refinement of this thesis Mark Griffith (2002) suggests that a male audience would oscillate between identification with the satyrs and heroes such as Odysseus.

Aeschylus was celebrated by the ancients for the quality of his satyr plays, which makes their loss all the more regrettable. (Podlecki 2005 provides a useful analysis of the fragments of Aeschylean satyr drama.) One common feature of satyr drama is the eventual overthrow of some form of monster, the Cyclops in Euripides' play, and the Sphinx presumably in Aeschylus' play. The same actors who had played the roles of Eteocles and the messenger took the roles of Oedipus and the Sphinx. The same chorus who performed in the *Seven* abandoned the role of frightened maidens fearing sexual violation to become satyrs who were notorious for their unrestrained sexuality.

Aeschylus and the Third Actor

Tragedy began as a drama performed by one actor in dialogue with the chorus. According to Aristotle it was Aeschylus who introduced the second actor. It was the responsibility of the state to fund actors, and since there were three poets competing at the City Dionysia, and two at the Lenaea, increasing the number of actors was a matter of civic concern—the Archon who authorized these expenses would be audited at the end of his term. Obviously at some point it was decided that each playwright could have three actors, an advance that Aristotle attributes to Sophocles (*Poetics* 1449a). The innovation changed tragedy profoundly, as the analysis of Sophocles' *Oedipus Tyrannus* in the next chapter will demonstrate.

Evidently Sophocles, whose career began in 468 (when he took first prize in a contest that included Aeschylus), had managed to convince the Archon to accept this new expense before 458. This is the date of its earliest use, not by Sophocles (whose first plays are lost to us), but by Aeschylus in his *Oresteian* trilogy. It would be difficult to improve on Bernard Knox's evaluation (1972: 107): "Aeschylus, almost at the end of a great career, was presented, willy-nilly, with a new instrument—an old dog obliged to learn new tricks." The following remarks are indebted to his perceptive analysis.

What this "old dog" did with his new trick was quite different from Sophocles' realistic three-way conversations. Granted, the third play of the trilogy, *Eumenides*, has three speaking actors on stage simultaneously: Apollo, Athena, and Orestes at his trial for homicide in Athens. But it is quite unlike the triangulated conversations that take place in *Oedipus*; indeed Orestes speaks very little during the scene. It is in the first two plays of the trilogy that Aeschylus uses his third actor (*tritagonist*) in a pair of *coups de théâtre* unparalleled in extant tragedy. In *Agamemnon* there are never three actors speaking in the same scene, but instead Aeschylus brings on a third actor to play the role of Cassandra, the Trojan priestess, whom Agamemnon leads into the acting space when he returns to Clytemnestra. The captive woman remains silent through the long homecoming scene as Clytemnestra persuades her husband to walk on the precious tapestries that she has laid at his feet. Even though Clytemnestra commands Cassandra to enter the house, the enslaved princess remains outside, still silent, while the chorus sings a short song of dread and confusion. Aeschylus was famous for his silent characters, and at this point an audience might have assumed that she was one of them. But then she starts to shriek and, in a series of lyrics and then spoken words, she describes her terrible visions, the ghosts of the children of Thyestes, and the imminent death of Agamemnon. It is a long and powerfully emotional scene and takes the chorus (and no doubt the audience) completely by surprise.

The actor playing the role of Cassandra obviously had a strong singing voice, but in the second play, *Choephori* ("Libation Bearers"), the third actor has but two lines, although important ones. He plays the role of Pylades, Orestes' constant companion, who stands by silently during a reconciliation scene with Electra, the siblings' eerie invocation of the dead Agamemnon, and eventually the confrontation between Orestes and Clytemnestra. As the young man wavers from his matricidal task, he turns to Pylades, who speaks his only two lines with oracular authority to remind Orestes of his oaths to Apollo to avenge his father's death (900–1).

This was the state of the art after four decades of development: the playwright had three actors, who, with the aid of masks and costumes, could play multiple roles; the chorus continued to be an important presence in the drama, not only in its songs and dances, but also its interactions with the characters; and the *skene* building had become incorporated in the dramatic space. We turn now to Sophocles' deployment of these elements in his most famous play.

3

The Mature Form: Sophocles' *Oedipus*

If tragedy, "undergoing many changes, stopped when it attained its own nature," as Aristotle determines (*Poet.* 1449a16), then Sophocles' *Oedipus Tyrannus* exemplifies its fulfillment. Since there is no secure external source for its date—a premiere between 430 and 425 BCE seems most likely—it is difficult to assess its precise position in the history of the genre, much less the "many changes" that preceded it. Although there are large gaps in the continuum, the vague outlines of the evolution of tragedy may still be discernible, although even the earliest of surviving Sophoclean tragedy represents the mature form of the drama. *Ajax*, to judge from its style and meter (for example the use of anapests in the prologue, Stanford 1963: 294), was produced around 447 BCE, nearly two decades before *Oedipus* and a decade after Aeschylus' *Oresteia*. The drama deals with events immediately after the Trojan War: the weapons of Achilles have been granted to Odysseus, which enrages Ajax. Before the action begins, the aggrieved hero, maddened by the goddess Athena, slaughters the camp's livestock in the belief that he is killing his fellow Greeks who insulted him by denying him the honor he so fittingly deserved. After realizing his delusion and now deeply shamed, he commits suicide by falling on his sword, an event that requires the chorus to be sent out of the orchestra, a rare occurrence, and one that also defies the convention of not representing violence in the theater. Or does it? David Seale (1983: 165) is surely correct that the moment requires "a visual, not an imagined climax," but how this was accomplished in the original production is a perplexing crux of ancient Greek stagecraft. According to the scholiast (an ancient commentator), a late fifth- or fourth-century revival of the play earned the actor Timotheus the sobriquet "Slayer" because of his brilliant rendition of the suicide; in that production, at least, it was not left to the audience's imagination. By some irretrievable theatrical legerdemain Sophocles manages to have his hero's corpse remain, albeit covered by a shroud, thereby kept in view of the audience during the final third of the drama, while his family and colleagues argue about how to deal with it. Odysseus, Agamemnon, and Teucer (the brother of Ajax) make their respective cases. This is a three-actor play: somehow the protagonist has removed himself from the costume and mask of Ajax, which has now become a prop, and returns in another role, possibly as Odysseus (although probably as Teucer), adding a piquant irony to the final scene. Eventually his wife, Tecmessa, takes her place in the tableau, but since three speaking actors are already present, she is, as Kirk Ormand (1996) observes, "silent by convention." Ormand not only alludes to the three-actor rule, but also to the expectation that respectable women be silent in public. Yet Tecmessa, a captive bride of slave status, has had much to say before this. Earlier she had repeated Ajax's reprimand that "silence is a woman's greatest ornament" (293). In her final appearance her silence suggests a higher status, comparable to that of an Athenian wife, to correspond with the honor that will now be shown to Ajax, who will have a cult devoted to him.

As this brief survey suggests, far from being restricted by the conventions of his art, Sophocles pushes them to their limits and exploits them to their fullest potential to create suspense and surprise, while investing his drama with complex social meaning. His use of the third actor is not as fully developed in *Ajax* as in *Oedipus*, which features a triangulated conversation at the pivotal moment of the hero's downfall, but it certainly indicates how skillfully he can manipulate the tools at his disposal. This includes his use of space and materiality. Since these topics are integral to the meaning of *Oedipus*, they deserve our scrutiny. *Ajax* deploys the *skene* in a remarkable manner. It represents the tent of Ajax on the beaches of Troy. Within its enclosure Ajax has committed his slaughter; he emerges briefly in the prologue still elated. But when his senses return, he howls in shame and agony—no longer visible, but certainly audible from within. Tecmessa then reveals him to the chorus and the audience. This pitiful spectacle manifests by means of the *ekkyklema*, a wheeled platform rolled out of the *skene* to reveal an interior scene, so that inside becomes outside. But the spatiality of the tragedy becomes even more complex during the ceremonial suicide: with the chorus sent away, Ajax is entirely alone— except of course, for the thousands of spectators in the theater, who share an intensely personal moment with the isolated warrior. The private space that he has established for himself is juxtaposed on the very public, civic space of the audience, so that once again he becomes a spectacle. In *Oedipus* the dramatic space and its social meaning fluctuate and overlap in different ways, but ones that also accentuate a conflation of public and private.

Sophocles' *Oedipus*, selected by Aristotle to illustrate the ideal plot, placed second at the City Dionysia, losing to Aeschylus' nephew Philocles, author of at least a hundred plays, none of which survive. A surprising verdict, it testifies to all the ephemeral variables contributing to the success of a tragic production. Was the chorus poorly trained, the music mediocre, the acting lackluster, the costumes and masks substandard, or even the weather inclement on the day of its premiere? According to one theory, Philocles' victory could have been due to an imperfect mechanism that did not count all ten judges' votes (Marshall and van Willigenburg 2004). Even so, this suggests that at least some judges were more

impressed with Philocles' production than with Sophocles'.[1]
Be that as it may, scholars from antiquity onward have praised
the structure of *Oedipus*. The following discussion draws on
Aristotle's influential analysis of tragedy but also considers its
limitations. As we parse the elements of a fully developed plot,
it will become evident that the topic is inseparable from the
subtle characterization of its paradigmatic tragic hero.

A technical masterpiece, *Oedipus* (the title preserved by
Aristotle) exemplifies several significant developments in the
evolution of the genre. The first is the abandonment of the
trilogy format, as previously noted. Aeschylus' *Seven Against
Thebes* dealt with the same accursed family as Sophocles' play,
but so did the two preceding plays, which represented actions
of preceding generations that led to the crisis in Thebes.
The *didaskalia*, ancient lists of productions, attest to the
disconnection between the mythic tales treated in a playwright's
package once the trilogy format was abandoned. No doubt
these three separate story lines were linked thematically, and
the next chapter will work with more evidence in the case of
Euripides. Unfortunately *didaskalia* are not available for all
productions, including the package of plays that included
Oedipus. The play is, despite the loss of its accompanying two
tragedies and satyr play, obviously a discrete and complete
narrative. The tightly constructed plot reaches its denouement
with the intervention of the third actor (the *tritagonist*), an
important development in the genre. The preceding chapter
outlined how Aeschylus used this additional speaking actor in a
unique and spectacular way, and only in his *Oresteia*. Aristotle
claims that Sophocles is responsible for the innovation, a claim
that the anonymous *Life of Aeschylus* contradicts, attributing
it to the older poet. But these anonymous biographies should
be treated with skepticism, since they often draw on the
poets' work as evidence for their lives (Lefkowitz 1981).
Regardless of whether he was the first to use the *tritagonist*,
however, it is obvious that Sophocles integrates him in a more
realistic manner than his predecessor did. Thus a three-way

conversation allows a long obscured truth to be revealed and thereby brings the plot to its tragic completion.

Another consequence of the third actor is a diminution of the role of the chorus, although as Aristotle notes (*Poet.*1456a) Sophoclean choruses are still more characters in their own right than are Euripidean choruses. The chorus of *Oedipus* is comprised of Theban elders who advise their king and are steadfastly loyal to him. They are less involved in the stage action than the chorus of distraught virgins in *Seven Against Thebes*, although their odes function as theological comments on the action. As we have seen, the chorus' fears expressed in the parodos of *Seven* led directly to the protagonist's interaction with them in the first episode. Although the *coryphaeus* of *Oedipus* interacts with the king, and functions as a witness to the drama, there is nothing to compare with the tense exchange between Eteocles and the chorus leader in the first episode of the earlier play. This phenomenon has an effect on the organization of the following discussion (and that of the next chapter). For the sake of continuity, we will survey the development of the plot without interruptions for a discussion of the choral songs. This is not to imply that the choral odes are disconnected from the action of the play, but there is a benefit to considering them as a unit in order to understand the progression of thought. This arrangement allows for a more tightly focused discussion of the design of the plot and articulation of the character of Oedipus.

Although Aristotle's assessment of tragedy has been subject to criticism and revision, it nonetheless provides a familiar nomenclature and useful departure point for an analysis of the relationship between plot and character in the play. Aristotle is less interested in the visual elements (*opsis*) of tragedy, but it is crucial to integrate the production components of *Oedipus* in an analysis of its meaning. To that end we consider some of the elements, both architectural and dramaturgical, that contribute to the arresting representation of Oedipus' inevitable catastrophe. *Oedipus*, like all extant tragedy after

Aeschylus' *Oresteia*, used the *skene* for actors' entrances and exits. Aristotle claims that Sophocles introduced *skenographia* "scene painting," although what that entailed is up for debate. The *skene* representing a royal palace in Sophocles' *Oedipus* is, like that of Aeschylus' *Agamemnon*, invested with a psychological depth and symbolic significance, but one that develops and changes throughout the drama. The intersections between the spaces represented in the theater with invisible spaces inside the *skene*, and those beyond the city, are an important element of the play. We will also be exploring how Sophocles, like Aeschylus, adds tension to the perceivable events in the mortal world by giving voice to an unseen dimension that undergirds the tangible humanity represented in the theater, the "dark matter" that manifests as oracles and coincidences, interlocking forces that contribute to the plot.

An aspect of the study of this play that cannot be ignored is the ancient audience, whose lived experiences guided their reception of the play. Sophocles' play, although set in Thebes, contains elements of Athenian homicide law and procedure, familiar to its original audience, that add texture to the action. Furthermore, the vivid description of the plague in the early part of the play had a special significance for the Athenian audience who had lived through the devastating disease that wiped out a quarter of their population (430–427 BCE). Robin Mitchell-Boyask (2008: 64–6) has argued that Sophocles did not take first prize with his *Oedipus* because it aligned too closely with the lives of the Athenian audience, who had suffered through the recent plague. The historian Thucydides (2.47.3) describes how the *nosos* "swooped down" upon Athens; Sophocles likewise refers to the plague in the same terms (e.g., *Oedipus* 28). Did he cut too close to the bone for the tastes of Athenian judges?

While these familiar events and circumstances contributed to the ancient reception of this tragedy, it continues to resonate widely with contemporary audiences. The final section of this chapter looks at a sample of recent productions of this provocative drama.

Sophocles and the Myth of Oedipus

The story that continues to spark our fascination goes back to the earliest surviving Greek literature: according to Homer, Odysseus sees the spirit of Oedipus' mother among the dead in Hades (11.271). Iconographic evidence suggests an increased interest during the sixth century in the Theban saga; epic poetry (the lost *Thebaid*) treats other episodes in his story, including Oedipus' confrontation with the Sphinx, the topic of Aeschylus' satyr drama (Torres-Guerra 2015). The narrative of his parricide and incest circulated in many forms, for example tragedies such as the now lost *Oedipus* of Sophocles' rival Philocles, produced on a different occasion. Episodes of the family's history featured in other lost tragedies including Aeschylus' *Oedipus*. Euripides treated the aftermath of Oedipus' discovery in *Phoenician Women* (*c*.410–408 BCE), which survives and includes a brief account of his crimes; Sophocles' final production, *Oedipus at Colonus* (401 BCE), the last surviving specimen of tragedy, written when the poet was in his nineties and produced after his death, dramatizes the final hours of the wandering exile. *Antigone,* one of his earliest plays, treated the subsequent suicide of his defiant daughter. Sophocles' original audience was well acquainted with Oedipus' biography; the basic elements of the tale were traditional. But it always bears remembering the elastic nature of myth: the poet put his own stamp on the story—the plague for example was probably his own contribution—although given the small selection of all versions of the myth it is difficult to ascertain the full extent of his innovations.

One of his more obvious decisions was to suppress any allusion to a curse that Laius would be killed by his own child, although he does make Oedipus utter a curse against the unknown murderer, which of course is himself. The epic *Thebaid*, surviving only in fragments, presents the workings of an inherited ancestral curse on the sons of Oedipus. The hypothesis to *Seven Against Thebes*, which echoes certain details from Euripides' *Phoenician Women*, provides some background: Laius raped the young son of Pelops, Chrysippus; Pelops subsequently cursed Laius and his descendants. Despite the Delphic oracle's warning not to beget a son, Laius gets drunk and impregnates Jocasta. The oracle and curse are thus intrinsically linked in these accounts, as they are in the hypothesis to Sophocles' *Oedipus*.[2] Our play, however, only highlights the oracle; details about the curse of Pelops are ignored. While an ancient audience could have been aware of the tradition of the curse, its influence over events in Sophocles' play is never stated.[3] In his careful analysis N. J. Sewell-Rutter (2007: 126–8) emphasizes the absence of any reference to the curse targeting Pelops in *Oedipus* and effectively dismantles suggestions that Sophocles' audience would have assumed the operations of an inherited curse. Instead, his version turns on the emotions, character, and intellect of his tragic hero to such an extent that Oedipus, despite the oracle's apparent force, appears to be the agent of his own downfall. Knox's (1975: 3–14) influential treatment of the play rebuts the idea espoused by Freud and others that this is a "tragedy of fate" and focuses instead on Oedipus' agency and choices. Nonetheless a few coincidences, which we might be inclined to attribute to the god, circumscribe that agency.

The playwright's treatment of the familiar tale is structured so precisely that it succeeds in creating a combination of suspense, fascination, and pathos, never diminished by our knowledge of how it will end. As in several of his other tragedies, such as *Women of Trachis*, Sophocles emphasizes the limitations of human understanding that lead to catastrophe. In that play, Deianeira uses what she thinks is a love potion to restore her husband Heracles' affections. It is actually a deadly poison; he dies in agony, thus fulfilling an oracle that predicted either his death or the end of his labors after fifteen months; both outcomes are one and the same. The most ironic use of oracular predictions, however, is in *Oedipus*. Oedipus' ignorance of his own identity skews his attempt to thwart an oracle that prophesizes the horrible events of his life. He has just enough information to ensure that he fulfills the prediction he tries to avoid: that he will kill his father and marry his mother. Apollo's oracle seems to be as much a cause as a prediction of catastrophe. The plot is constructed so seamlessly that Oedipus' movement toward knowledge is, within the compass of the drama, a product of his own volition; this is a character-driven narrative. The invisible presence of Apollo and Zeus notwithstanding, everything that happens is a result of a decision made by Oedipus. David Kovacs (2009) uses the analogy of a chess master competing against an ordinary player. The master says he is going to win in a certain number of moves, but not exactly how. Likewise Apollo has predicted that Oedipus will kill his father and marry his mother but leaves it to Oedipus to make the moves. In situating his hero between divine power and mortal agency, Sophocles has fashioned one of the subtlest and most psychologically nuanced characters in extant Greek tragedy. The effect of Oedipus' personality on the action of the play is correspondingly complex. Indeed that personality is so embedded in the structure of the plot that it is impossible to discuss one without the other.

This brings us back to Aristotle who identifies tragedy as the "imitation of an action" with plot and character as constitutive elements. According to Aristotle, Sophocles claimed that he depicted people "as they should be," while Euripides depicted them as they are. Aristotle approves of Sophocles' representation of character, which he likens to that of Homer: a tragic hero should be *spoudios* "good," "noble," or "serious" (*Poet.* 1448a). Correspondingly a tragedy should represent action that is "serious" (*spoudios*), "complete," and possessing "magnitude." By imitation (*mimesis*) of such an action, tragedy accomplishes "through pity and fear, the catharsis [a much debated term that probably denotes a kind of emotional release] of such emotions" (1448b). Later in the *Poetics*, Aristotle considers the *peripeteia*, reversal of fortune, which is due to a *hamartia*, not a character flaw but a mistake due to lack of knowledge, which is certainly the case with Oedipus. Nonetheless there are inevitable questions. Why did Oedipus marry a woman old enough to be his mother after an oracle predicted he would marry his mother? Why, since he had killed an older man, did he not realize that he was the killer of Laius? Sophocles' text provides answers, as we shall see, but also delineates an intricate web of unknown, and unknowable, forces that dovetail with the meticulously portrayed personality and emotions of his hero.

Gordon Kirkwood (1955: 55–6), in a rudimentary schematization influenced by Aristotle, categorizes Sophoclean drama into two groups. The first features a diptych plot, which deals with two characters whose fates intersect: for example, the efforts of the young Greek warrior Neoptolemus to bring the exiled Philoctetes back from Lemnos to the Trojan War. The second deploys a linear plot that focuses on a single character. *Oedipus* exemplifies this category: its plot is driven by the actions and character of its protagonist and his interactions with the citizens of Thebes, his family members, and finally, and most significantly, a former household slave. Even in those rare moments of his absence, Oedipus is the focus of every conversation; when present he engages vigorously with every character in his orbit. These interpersonal dynamics demonstrate the elements of his character within the scope of the drama but also reflect details of his past actions that led to the present crisis.

Kirkwood writes admiringly of his heroic qualities: his matchless intellect and genuine concern for the suffering of the Theban people. But William Scott (1996) is not so sanguine. In his estimation, Oedipus is restrictive and controlling right from the opening moments of the play and grows increasingly tyrannical as the plot unfolds. That two such readings of the same character can coexist testifies to the richness of Sophocles' portrait, its complexity already evident in the prologue.

Structure and Themes

Prologue

A priest leads forth a cluster of townspeople, young and old, carrying branches wreathed with raw wool, implements of the supplication ritual; they take their abject positions before the *skene* door and the altars before the palace. The door opens, Oedipus comes forth, and the play begins. When he addresses the suppliants, he acknowledges the rituality of the space but also charges it with a civic energy that is curiously personal at the same time. The first words of the drama are his, *o tekna* ("children"), simultaneously a solicitous expression of his deep concern, a disturbing reminder of the issues of parentage that undergird the drama, and an example of the conflation of public and private identity that defines Oedipus. He continues to address his afflicted subjects as *tekna* throughout the remainder of the prologue. "Why are you here?" he asks them.

The priest of Zeus, god of suppliants, conveys the confidence that the suffering population have in their king. They believe that the man who had saved their city by solving the riddle of the Sphinx will find an answer to another enigma, the mysterious plague that has descended upon them, blighting crops and livestock, killing women in childbirth, and rendering infants stillborn. And they are right: indeed he has anticipated their petition, having recently sent his wife's brother, Creon, to the Delphic oracle for an explanation of the devastation and a solution. Thus in less than a hundred lines, the play conveys several essential, interlaced aspects of Oedipus' character: he is profoundly concerned with doing the right thing for his people, whose pain is his pain, and he is a "fixer," who uses his analytical powers for civic good.

Creon arrives, as if on cue, to deliver the oracle's pronouncement: the plague is the result of *miasma*, the psychic pollution caused by the unresolved homicide of Laius. The Delphic revelation replicates a very real concern of Athenian homicide procedure that anchors the play in its audience's own experience. The fifth-century orator Antiphon, writing around the time this play was produced, warns of the communal danger of having a killer at large: "the entire polis is defiled by him, until he is prosecuted" (2.1.3). Understanding the cause of the plague, Oedipus now takes matters into his own hands, another display of astute judgment and executive ability; he considers himself to be "the land's avenger" (135), working together with the god. And he sets the investigation on its course.

On the other hand, the prologue also hints at less commendable personality traits, growing more palpable in the course of the drama. Scott (1996: 123) argues that the characteristic response of Oedipus in the first half of the play is "to constrain and control." This is evident when he disrupts the suppliants' rituals by sending them home and summons the leading citizens, represented by the chorus. He becomes, in effect, a temporary director of the play, determining when the prologue ends and the parodos begins. As the drama unfolds, his ability to supervise other characters' comings and goings diminishes, although his efforts to control the action do not. But for now, in accordance with his command, the priest and suppliants depart; the chorus enters singing a prayer that the gods will deliver their city from the pestilence. The text gives no indication that Oedipus left the acting space, which may well be one of the rare cases when a character's exit is not indicated by another (Taplin 1977: 284).

First Episode

Characters do not always seem aware of choral songs: but like Eteocles in the *Seven Against Thebes*, Oedipus acknowledges the chorus's concerns. Supremely confident in his own power, he declares that if they listen to his words they will find relief from the disease. The chorus prayed to the gods; Oedipus seemingly accepts their prayers. A man of action, he immediately issues a proclamation that a fifth-century Athenian audience would recognize from their own homicide procedures. It includes a curse on the killer and anyone who harbors him or them. His edict banning the killer from public spaces echoes the proclamation by the Athenian Archon Basileus ("King Archon"), the elected official who initiated a homicide investigation and presided over it: echoes of Athenian homicide procedure in his edict have been identified by Ed Carawan (1999), a scholar of ancient Greek law. Not only has Oedipus performed the role of the magistrate who launches the investigation, he also takes on, without knowing it, the role of the closest male relative who, according to Athenian law, was responsible for carrying out the investigation. It was the duty of this kinsman, as prescribed by the law of Draco, to publically announce his intention to bring the killer to trial and prosecute him or her in court. In a sense that is exactly what Oedipus does, unsuspectingly enacting the role of the nearest kinsman.

Thus his proclamation, capped by a curse, adds another layer of social meaning, the juridical, to the physical space of the theater; it is also an implicit acknowledgment of public and private identities integral to Athenian homicide law. This ancient law attributed to the sixth-century lawgiver Draco was so efficiently drafted that it remained intact during the fifth century; carved into rotating wooden columns, it was available to anyone who needed to consult it. Sophocles' audience would know it well. When the chorus leader swears that he "did not do the killing, nor can reveal who did" (276–9), he echoes the oaths made by witnesses in Athenian homicide trials. Echoes of the venerable homicide law of Athens thus identify Oedipus as a good ruler, but his proclamation is also, as Oedipus himself soon acknowledges, a self-curse.

The religious and the legal were compatible modalities in ancient Greek thought. Homicide procedures, in particular, had ritual components including the network of oaths performed during the investigation and trial. The court of the Areopagus, as dramatized in Aeschylus' *Eumenides*, was established and presided over by the goddess Athena, one of many examples of the divine origins of law. Adding to the religious texture of this scene, the chorus leader suggests that Oedipus should consult the seer Tiresias, whose mantic arts might provide some clarification. Once again Oedipus demonstrates his executive skills, having already summoned the blind prophet (289). And, as if to demonstrate the authority and efficiency of the king,

Tiresias makes his entrance forthwith, led by a boy. Oedipus is, throughout the play, a ruler whose commitment to seeking the truth apparently puts him one step ahead of everyone else. Clearly this is a king whose executive decisions demonstrate that he is an exemplary ruler.

But such unequivocal admiration for Oedipus only takes us so far. He is after all only a man, the "greatest of men," as the priest had put it in the prologue (14–55), but not a god, as he immediately qualifies. And his all too human frailty, specifically the emotions that limit and distort his perception of reality, becomes evident as he interacts with Tiresias. The old man reluctantly tells him that *he* is the "defiled criminal": the term *miastor* is a potent condemnation, implying a contagious psychic pollutant. Oedipus is enraged by the bald accusation, although he had pressured Tiresias for insight and Tiresias only came with great reluctance. And so Sophocles reveals another facet of Oedipus' complex character. Why does this intelligent man, solver of riddles, resist the truth? For one thing, he is working with flawed evidence. The priest had reported that Laius was killed by "robbers." The chorus leader again uses the plural: "It was said that he died at the hands of wayfarers." Jocasta will repeat the story later. Hearsay—there are no eyewitnesses to the crime in Thebes, as Oedipus observes, although he will soon send for the sole survivor of the homicide. But his subtle mind comes up with another reason to doubt Tiresias: the seer could not solve the riddle of the Sphinx; clearly his prophetic powers are limited. Working with available information, he tries to piece it all together, concluding that Tiresias and Creon are conspiring against him.

At this point we catch a whiff of Oedipus' limitations: he is given to rage, *orgē*, a word repeated throughout the scene. It is an emotion Oedipus detects in Tiresias, who responds by calling out Oedipus' anger (*you* criticize my *orgē*, 337); the chorus leader identifies the *orgē* of both men (405). This emphasis provides an immediate correspondence to the past, when two angry men also confronted each other. The fury that erupts in this first episode, and in the next, corresponds to the rage that overcame Oedipus beset by Laius and his retinue at the crossroads. At that time his fury was so powerful, practically superhuman, that he killed the entire cortege (save the one, who escaped undetected). Ironically, at the moment of his most vehement denial, Oedipus displays the facet of his character that led to his crime.

After this angry exchange, Oedipus tries to dismiss Tiresias, but the prophet has the last word and without equivocation tells Oedipus the whole truth, that the man "whom you seek, with threats and proclamations, the killer of Laius, this man is here, a foreigner, called an immigrant, but one who will be revealed as Theban born" (448). He had already claimed that Oedipus was the killer; now he goes further to predict his blindness, "going with a staff" (*skeptrōi*, 456), and to describe his incest and the children born of that incest. And Oedipus, who until now had determined who came and left (and is probably moving toward the palace door), is scornfully dismissed by the prophet: "go inside and think things over" (461). The old man then leaves, led by the boy, but on his own terms. And so the episode that opened with a civic edict ends with an oracular proclamation that emphasizes the ignorance and fallibility of the king whose secular power and authority have started to crumble even as he begins his pursuit of the truth. The chorus, whose leader has tried to mediate the dispute, now sings its first stasimon, and it is evident that although the audience understands Tiresias to be identifying Oedipus' parricide and incest, they have no idea of the truth.

Second Episode

Oedipus' prime suspect is Creon, whom he has accused of collaborating with Tiresias to depose him, just as he had, according to this logic, deposed Laius by more violent means. His hypothesis is not irrational: Creon urged him to consult the oracle in the first place; Creon delivered the oracle's pronouncement regarding the cause of the *miasma*; Tiresias subsequently points the finger at Oedipus. It looks to Oedipus, that solver of riddles, like a set-up. The accusation of conspiracy has been made publically in the very space before the palace where Oedipus had received the suppliant citizens. And it takes very little time for it to reach the accused. The second episode opens with the entrance of Creon, insulted and defensive. Again the chorus leader tries to mitigate a volatile situation, suggesting that their king spoke in anger (*orgei*) rather than with sense (522). Oedipus now returns from within the palace (as Creon observes, 531), his rage still flaring. He has had time to let his suspicions marinate, and it now seems to him that Creon is plotting a second regicide, this one against *him* (534). The implication is that if the conspirators can make him seem guilty of murder, they would have him executed. And while this notion is far off the mark, it is entirely understandable, as long as Oedipus remains unaware of who he is and the true circumstances of the murder of Laius.

Creon has a rebuttal at the ready: he is perfectly content with his position in the Theban political hierarchy, which gives him power and prestige without the envy of the populace. Like a defendant in a homicide case he swears an oath of denial, which Oedipus refuses to accept. He is so confident of his blamelessness that he invites Oedipus to go to Delphi himself, but Oedipus will not let go of his anger and suspicions. Most tragedy features some type of confrontation, or *agon* ("contest"), that like this one involves an intense exchange of stichomythia. We saw an example in the first episode of Aeschylus' *Seven Against Thebes*, although in that case the confrontation was between Eteocles and the *coryphaeus*. Here the debate conveys the extreme agitation of Oedipus, which steadily increases. Even when Creon presents a rational argument explaining why he is content with his current status, and despite the affirmation by the *coryphaeus* that Creon has "spoken well" (616), Oedipus will not give up the idea of a conspiracy.

The heated altercation outside the palace advances the plot. The fracas is loud enough to reach Jocasta within; she enters from the *skene* and, much like a mother breaking up a boys' quarrel, remonstrates with the two men. "You, go inside," (637) she commands the man who is, unbeknownst to all, her son. He remains in order to explain his anger. Her response, intended to sooth, instead sets his thoughts churning. Jocasta has no use for prophets: an oracle foretold that a child of Laius would kill his father. Instead the former king was attacked by foreign highwaymen "where the three roads meet." Moreover, Laius had bound the feet of their infant son, not yet three days old, and put him "into the hands of another" to be cast out on the "trackless mountain" (716–18)—so much for mantic utterances. But the mention of the three roads alarms Oedipus, who presses for details, and his anxiety only deepens upon hearing the precise location of the crime: in the land of Phocis where the road leading to Delphi forks. And the time of the killing was only shortly before Oedipus arrived in Thebes. Ironically Laius was en route to the very oracle that Oedipus was leaving, the oracle that had predicted his parricide and incest. Oedipus' thoughts are in turmoil, but he presses Jocasta for details. "What was his physique? At what stage of youth was he?" (740–1). The second part of the question is oddly worded, as if to avoid asking whether Laius was an older man, like the one he had killed.

Her response does not reassure: "Black hair just beginning to turn white, and he was not much different from you in appearance" (742–3). Oedipus is now all but convinced that he killed Laius. Nonetheless he presses forward with unflagging determination, ordering the only survivor of the slaughter to be summoned. After a series of incisive questions, he has nearly solved the crime and requires only the substantiation of the slave who asked to be sent beyond the city when he returned to find Oedipus as its new king. The pacing of Sophocles' plot is impeccable; he now pauses the action for a flashback. It remains for the audience to learn the details of Oedipus' past from the man himself. What led him to that life-changing fork in the road?

Oedipus, in an eighty-line narrative *rhesis* (a speech in iambic trimeters), apprises his wife (and thus the audience) of a dramatic series of events in his past. The account bears similarities with messenger speeches, a standard feature of tragedy.[4] Occurring at the halfway point of the play, it makes everything else in the drama seem to radiate outward from this nexus of events. Oedipus' tale has the temporary effect of stalling the action, revealing the past in vivid detail, all in the form of a journey that led to this present moment. This narrative, the genetic code of the drama, so to speak, is not only the prequel to his current situation, but also a resumé of the character traits that led to it. As a young Corinthian prince, son of Polybus and Merope, Oedipus was considered to be "the greatest man" of Corinth (776), just as he is currently "the first of men" in Thebes (33). A drunkard at a banquet taunts him as the fraudulent child of his father. He questions his parents closely—this is the same Oedipus who relentlessly grills Tiresias, his wife, and eventually the witness to the homicide. Ignoring his parents' angry denials, he visits the Delphic oracle, just as intent on learning the facts then as he is now and just as intractable to the arguments of others (in this case Polybus and Merope). Correspondingly, his first response is to consult the same expert advisor as he did in the first moments of this tragedy when confronted with a different crisis or rather a different manifestation of the same crisis. Instead of answering the question of his parentage, however, the Pythia stated that

> I was fated to have intercourse with my mother, and to reveal a family unbearable for human eyes to see, and that I would be the killer of the father who begat me.
>
> (791–3)

Oedipus' younger self chooses to avoid this revolting fate by never returning to Corinth, a precaution that immediately fulfills the third line of the prophecy. In a narrow passage, the very spot Jocasta just described, he is pushed aside by the belligerent driver of the cortege; Oedipus in turn struck him "in anger" (*orgei*), and then his passenger, who struck him. Oedipus now confesses that he killed "the lot of them" with his staff (*skeptrōi*) "by this right hand" (811–13).

The scepter is a universal symbol of authority, often referred to as such in Greek poetry. Stage properties are relatively rare in Greek tragedy, a rarity that emphasizes them when they do appear (Taplin 1977: 77). This play, like most of tragedy, requires very few; the suppliant boughs placed on the altars in the prologue are the most obvious. Sofer (2003: 3) describes a prop as "an object that goes on a journey," in other words, something beyond a scene-setting object, but rather an item freighted with denser semiotic value. Only one object in this play conforms to this criterion in that its semiotic function changes over the course of the drama. The scepter in his hand "goes on a journey" when Oedipus recounts his violent encounter with Laius and his retinue at the narrow passage where the three roads meet. In response to Laius' blow, Oedipus killed him (811–13) "by this here hand with my scepter." Ruby Blondell's translation (2002) conveys this more elegantly as "by this staff in my hand."[5] There are other words for a walking stick—*rhabdos* or *baktron*—and while *skeptros* works just as well, it also denotes kingly authority. If Oedipus is holding a scepter when he recounts the killings—as would be likely for a king—the effect is that he is holding the murder weapon. A benign accessory of royal power suddenly transforms into a deadly bludgeon. The object in his hand thus connects past and present in the most visceral manner possible.

As he surmises, if that man at the crossroads was Laius, then he has, only moments ago in his proclamation, cursed himself and must go into exile. And yet he cannot return to Corinth since he still fears the fulfillment of the oracle. After this interlude in the dramatic action—a long-buried memory of a disturbing and violent history—Oedipus resumes his investigation. His only solace is that according to the eyewitness Laius was killed by a band of highwaymen, not one man. Oedipus is under the impression that he killed the entire retinue, with no survivors; he repeats his request that the sole survivor be summoned. The plot is in high gear; Oedipus and Jocasta exit into the palace; the chorus sings a short second stasimon.

Third Episode

The third episode begins unexpectedly with Jocasta returning alone outside, bearing wreathes and incense to offer to Apollo. Two acts of supplication, involving similar gestures and objects, define the two parts of the play. But the supplication that opened the prologue was on behalf of the suffering Thebans in the city beyond. Jocasta's ritual act is the consequence of the worries and anxieties of Oedipus, who remains within the *skene*, letting his emotions, according to Jocasta, rise "too high" (914). The focus of the first half of the play has been entirely on the area outside the palace, throughout the city or beyond its limits, but the *skene* has become very intriguing at this point, standing as a container for, or even a symbol of, the turbulent thoughts of Oedipus. And the focus of the drama has telescoped, so that the very public nature of the first half of the play has been replaced by the personal concerns of Oedipus, who remains inside, and those of Jocasta, who now leaves him within as she seeks to intercede with Apollo on his behalf. The shift in Oedipus' role here—in the prologue the supplication is to him, here it is on his behalf—is a concise index of his diminishing control of events. Jocasta's appeal to Apollo may seem a striking contrast to her recent dismissal of oracles, but she is not a sacrilegious woman, only one who is not convinced that human agents can interpret the ways of the gods. What she appeals for is quite specific, "a release from this defilement" (921), precisely what the Theban suppliants had asked for earlier. Her concern, however, is not the suffering polis, but rather its leader, who seems like "a ship's helmsman stricken with panic" (923).

And then a second unexpected entrance: a man from Corinth arrives as if in answer to Jocasta's prayer. Naturally an audience would be expecting the witness to the murder of Laius at this point in fulfillment of the king's command. Until now Oedipus had only to say the word and the person summoned would appear, first Creon with the oracle, then the chorus, and then

Tiresias. Instead, completely unanticipated, a messenger arrives with the news that Polybus is dead, and the citizens expect Oedipus to return as king. Jocasta sends for him; now it is Oedipus who enters in response to a summons. Husband and wife agree that oracles are useless, since he obviously did not kill Polybus, but Oedipus still has anxieties about sleeping with his mother. What happens next, we would call a coincidence; for the ancients it would be *tychē*, a term that includes luck, or chance, sometimes understood as divine intervention. For the poet Hesiod (*Theogony* 360), *Tychē* is a goddess, one of the oldest. Herodotus, who often seems Sophoclean in his version of historical events, is partial to representing kings whose downfalls are the result of happenstance. Writing on the operation of *tychē* in this play, Charles Segal (1981: 44) observes that in Greek thought royalty "is bound especially closely to the wheel of fortune and is especially vulnerable to its sudden turns." At the end of this episode Oedipus will describe himself as a "child of *Tychē*," an accurate assessment, although not for the reason he thinks. As *Tychē* would have it then, here is the same man who received the ill-fated infant from the Theban slave on Mount Cithaeron and presented him to Polybus and Merope. His assurance that Oedipus need have no fear of sex with his mother has a devastating effect on Jocasta, who only moments before had scoffed at the oracle's prediction of Oedipus' incest and now immediately recognizes its truth. Her final moments of life are dedicated to trying to persuade the man she recognizes as her son to recant his order to interrogate that slave, the very man to whom she gave her newborn son. Failing in this futile attempt, she enters the *skene* for the last time. Oedipus misunderstands her revulsion: "a high and mighty woman, she feels shame at my lowly origins" (1078–9). In the last few minutes before the scales fall from his eyes, he looks forward to learning of his birth, a shift in focus from the murder investigation. The chorus sings a short optimistic ode, speculating about their king's divine birth, while the actor playing Jocasta changes mask and costume inside the *skene*.

Fourth Episode

That actor now returns from the *eisodos* in the role of the Theban shepherd, the eyewitness summoned by Oedipus, to deliver the truth Jocasta had vainly tried to suppress. Oedipus plunges ahead as persistently as ever to solve this new mystery of his origins, apparently diverted from the homicide investigation, although that mystery too is about to be solved. There is a legal timbre to the space when he interrogates this cringing slave. Let us assume that he is still holding his kingly scepter, which now might call to mind the juridical staff, held by *dikastai*, citizen-judges in Athenian courts. Oedipus orders his attendants to twist back the Theban herdsman's hands, a threat of physical violence that the audience would understand was necessary: in Athenian courts slave testimony was only acceptable if obtained by torture. The interview uses a series of stichomythia exchanged between the three characters, a most compelling example of the device, to create a rapid-fire interrogation of a reluctant witness. The episode is short, essential, and devastating.

The force of this scene and its contribution to the plot derive from a previous relationship between the two shepherds, one from the household of Laius, the other from Corinth. The slave witness arrives in answer to the summons of Oedipus; by a cruel twist of fate he is not only witness to the crime, but also the slave who handed the infant Oedipus to the Corinthian messenger. The brief episode is a superb example of how Sophocles uses the third actor, a convention long established but never deployed to such dramatic effect. The social dynamics between, and shared history of, the three men manifests as a triangulated conversation. Each participant engages with each of the other two men: the Theban slave of Laius trying desperately to withhold his knowledge, shrinking from the Corinthian messenger's insistent reminders, and relenting under Oedipus' brutal questioning; the Corinthian messenger, guileless, convinced that he is bringing good news, and doing a service to Oedipus, and then pressing the Theban to recall their previous meeting; Oedipus, bringing his force and authority to bear on that cowering slave. (These three-way conversations are less prominent in the earlier *Antigone* and *Ajax*, even though they use the *tritagonist*, which suggests that Sophocles developed the technique through the course of his career.)

Collectively these three actors from three different places embody the junction of those three roads, where Oedipus killed his father. The spatial dynamics are intensified by a sophisticated use of characters from three different but converging points meeting in the performance space: the Corinthian arrives from the *eisodos* that represents the space beyond the city, the Theban from the *eisodos* corresponding to the city, and Oedipus from the *skene* door. Rush Rehm (2002: 117–19) describes the conjunction as "drawing together the separate strands of Thebes, Corinth and Kithairon." And it is a reunion of sorts, although especially grim, of three individuals whose lives meshed together decades earlier on Mount Cithaeron. The space bristles with memory as it encompasses a re-enactment of the past.

After his brief interrogation of the reluctant slave, Oedipus now understands that he is the son of Jocasta and Laius and rushes into the palace to confront Jocasta. His *anagnorisis*, defined by Aristotle as a change from ignorance to knowledge, the recognition of his parricide and incest, coincides with his *peripeteia*, a tragic reversal from being the greatest man of Thebes to its most pathetic. This is the structure so admired by Aristotle (*Poet.* 1452a): the *anagnorisis*, "recognition," and *peripeteia*, "reversal," occur simultaneously and are seamlessly woven into the plot.

Exodus

After the chorus sings a stasimon reflecting on the mutability of fortune and the horror of incest, a messenger emerges from the palace to recount the events within. Messenger speeches were performances in and of themselves, with passages of direct discourse, and dramatic descriptions of violence. This one provides a vivid account of the horrific events within—the suicide of Jocasta and the self-mutilation of Oedipus. A particularly arresting feature is the emphasis on the rage of Oedipus against Jocasta: he bursts open the door to her chamber, ripping it off the wall, and finds her swinging from the ceiling. Tragic female characters' death by suicide is such a trope of the genre that Nicole Loraux (1987) devotes much of her monograph, *Tragic Ways of Killing a Woman*, to the phenomenon. Unlike the suicide of Ajax, a ritualistic self-immolation by sword, suicides in their bedchambers are the choice of women, most of them wives, in tragedy. Hanging is the typical feminine mode of death: Euripides' Phaedra, for example in *Hippolytus*. But when Oedipus comes upon his dead wife-mother, his rage at her softens and then turns on himself.

The final appearance of the polluted Oedipus deploys an unusual device to convey his new status. After the messenger's visceral and extensive description of Oedipus repeatedly piercing his eyeballs with Jocasta's gold fastening pins, and the bloody ooze streaming down his cheeks (1268–79), there must be some evidence of his self-mutilation. This is one of a few instances of a necessary change or modification of a mask in surviving tragedy.[6] The chorus' comment on his disfigured visage is a strong suggestion of this novel theatrical moment (1303–6). The change in Oedipus' fortunes and status are thus uniquely inscribed on his material being.

The messenger urges the doors to be unlocked to reveal the scene within; the spectacle calls for the *ekkyklema*.[7] If Oedipus was thus thrust forth from the *skene*, it would emphasize his connection with the interior spaces of the royal domicile, spaces that he tainted with his incest. Within the course of a day he has tumbled from his position as alpha male in the city of Thebes to an abject portrayal of defilement on a wheeled platform. Sophoclean tragedy has a predilection for representing its heroes in a disfigured or diseased state: Philoctetes is isolated because of a festering wound on his foot; Heracles makes his entrance in *Women of Trachis* in agony as the fatal garment corrodes his flesh; Ajax's affliction is psychological, but he commits suicide before the audience, and his massive corpse is visible throughout the second half of the play. Oedipus is brought low, to be sure, but a final humiliation awaits him.

To expunge the *miasma* from the city, he should go into exile, but Creon now makes his entrance (announced by the chorus, 1416) and insists that Oedipus return into the *skene* until the oracle has been consulted. Accordingly scholars have suspicions about the ending of the play. But it seems entirely appropriate that the king, so accustomed to others coming at his beck and call, should ultimately have his own comings and goings dictated by another.

The Chorus

In contrast to Aeschylean drama, which is on average at least 50 percent choral odes, Sophocles' odes comprise roughly 20 percent of the text.[8] The shape of the drama is now a more complex exchange between characters, epitomized by the triangulated interaction between two nameless minions and Oedipus. The addition of the third actor coincides with the reduced role of the chorus, which is nevertheless still an important element of Sophoclean tragedies. The *coryphaeus* engages in a meaningful way with every character in the play, all the while endorsing Oedipus in his position as king. Furthermore, the chorus leader's interaction with these characters is consistent with the thoughts expressed in the odes. Correspondingly the choral songs of *Oedipus*, among the most elegant of tragedy, reflect the elders' reaction to the events as they develop. Taken together they reveal a progression of thought that contemplates the relationship between the divine and mortal worlds.

Parodos

The chorus represents a group of respected Theban citizens (512, *andres politai*, in Creon's words) described by Jocasta as "lords of the land" (911). These elders personify the community, a common identity for the tragic chorus.[9] The parodos establishes their persona and reflects the concerns of the prologue with its description of the noxious effects of the plague. The efficacy of religion is a prevailing concern: the chorus enters while singing a paean, or prayer, that follows naturally from the priest's final plea in the prologue for salvation, although this choral prayer is addressed not to Apollo, surprisingly, but to Zeus. As Segal notices (1981: 22–3), Zeus figures prominently in their choral odes. This chorus plays an important mediating role between intersecting levels of ritual meaning (the religious aspects of the mythological/dramatic space and the religious beliefs of the audience). Their songs suggest a group of men with a firm base in religion who are attempting to develop a consistent response to the events in the episodes (Scott 1996: 126).

In the first episode Oedipus acknowledges their concerns directly, and his subsequent edict, cursing the murderers of Laius, is addressed to them in their role as citizens. The chorus displays a complex relationship with their king, acting in an advisory capacity, and lowering the emotional temperature when Oedipus engages in his altercations with Tiresias and Creon.

First Stasimon

The first stasimon (463–511), performed immediately after Tiresias' explicit accusations of incest and murder, meditates on the Delphic oracle, and the identity of the killer, whom the chorus envisions limping through the wilds like a bull. For a moment, they unwittingly predict Oedipus, whose name refers to his deformed feet, in exile among the mountains, and yet they can think of no reason to accept the prophet's words and conclude with a statement of support for Oedipus.

The First *Kommos*

The second episode features a complex lyric exchange between the chorus and Oedipus (and later Jocasta), who responds in song, a feature of tragedy known as a *kommos*. This one is also interspersed with spoken dialogue (649–96). The chorus does its best to restrain Oedipus' anger and expresses shock and disapproval at his refusal to accept Creon's oath of denial. The lyrics in the middle of this tense moment, an unusual device, draw attention to Oedipus' refusal to accept Creon's oath, an exceptional format for an exceptional behavior. Oedipus is still gravely concerned that a plot is underfoot to kill him, but he reluctantly agrees to spare Creon. After Creon's exit the chorus turns to Jocasta in another lyric exchange, creating a unique *kommos* in extant Sophoclean drama (Scott 1996: 131).

Second Stasimon

The second stasimon (863–910), performed shortly after Oedipus recounts killing Laius and his retinue, reflects the legal themes of the preceding episodes, but also the elders' focus on religious matters, thereby exemplifying the close conceptual association of these two social modalities. It is the subject of much debate. The ode is tightly organized with recurring themes augmented by verbal symmetry and an intricate metrical pattern that balances its apparently antithetical ideas.[10] Of course these complex thoughts would wash over an audience who would not necessarily be as punctilious as the classical philologists who parse their meaning. Some of these scholars suggest that the elders are processing Jocasta's rejection of oracles moments before; others that they are reacting to the disjunction between the oracle that Laius would be killed by his son and the evidence that he was not. The elders' allusive language allows for multiple interpretations.

The stanzas of choral odes are referred to as strophes, and antistrophes, their exact metrical double. The first strophe of this ode begins with the common notion that "high-stepping laws" come from the gods; they are "brought to life" in the heavens. The corresponding antistrophe turns to law's opposite, *hubris*, a legal and ethical term that denotes arrogant violence; it picks up the theme of begetting and birth, especially resonant for the story of Oedipus. "*Hubris* breeds the tyrant," proclaims the first line of this antistrophe, which carries on the imagery of the strophe.[11] There is a pun, of which the elders seem unaware: *Hubris* grasps for riches but gains "no foothold" *ou podi* (878), a contrast to "high stepping laws." But, is the chorus, so loyal to Oedipus, really thinking that his *hubris* made him king? The term *tyrannos* had a negative political valence for a democratic Athenian audience and is one reason why we refer to this play as *Oedipus Tyrannus*. But it is unlikely that the chorus is referring to their king. They remained supportive of Oedipus, even after the accusations of the seer. Oedipus in turn was respectful of their advice and refrained from action against Creon, although he had reason to believe the latter was plotting against him. While the elders' words apply to Oedipus, they remain devoted to him after the ode. To whom, then, does their term *tyrannos* refer? The best possible answer is no specific individual, but a type, as Chris Carey (1986: 177) suggests.[12]

The first antistrophe expands these themes by contemplating the actions of the hubristic man, which they compare to productive ambition. Oedipus seems to exemplify this latter category. But the next two stanzas (strophe and antistrophe B) move from the moral certitude of the first strophic pair: the chorus may wish that criminals are punished, but if they are not, "Why should I dance?" This remarkable question, a self-reflexive acknowledgment of their role in the tragic production, is also, less specifically, an indictment of the efficacy of ritual and its role in ensuring a secure moral order enforced by the gods.[13] If oracles are no longer true—as seems the oracle regarding Laius—then the gods are no longer interested in human morality and offer no guidance. And the conclusion of the final stanza reinforces this sentiment: "Things divine (i.e. religion) are flowing out."

Understandably, there is much controversy about the meaning of these lyrics. Does the chorus view the quarrel between Oedipus and Creon as a political upheaval that would give rise to *hubris*? Keith Sidwell points out (1992: 106–22) that the chorus has, until this point and thereafter, responded in some way to the action. He reads the ode as a specific attempt to exonerate Oedipus of Laius' killing. Yet interpretations that suggest a political meaning seem to strain the sense of these ambiguous lines. Carey reads the ode as a generalized anxiety, rather than a specific accusation of a political coup. This seems a better interpretation: the chorus is anxious and confused, but still loyal to Oedipus. Its ode sets the tone for the next episode when Jocasta comes forth to supplicate Apollo. Suffice to say, the meaning of the song was probably just as ambiguous to an ancient audience as it is to recent classicists. This magnificent but mysterious ode, the centerpiece of the drama's lyrics, sits between the first two choral prayers, which confirm the elders' faith in the gods' powers to keep their city safe, and the final two songs, which respectively convey first an optimistic speculation about the potentially divine origins of Oedipus and, after the revelation of his incest and parricide, a sober acceptance of the truth.

There is an obvious emotional trajectory, from fear, doubt, temporary optimism, and then repulsion, to these songs, even when their meanings are clouded. Segal offers the most sensible approach—and his comment applies equally well to some of the more difficult choral odes of tragedy. He views them as an example of a "thought-experiment" or "hypothesis about meaning rather than a final assertion of the play's meaning" (1981: 20). The elders are characters in the drama without complete knowledge of all the facts: they try to make sense of the troubling contradictions and suffering that they witness.

Yet, as Segal rightly observes, they can often articulate, without realizing, hidden forces and deeper meanings. They are both person and expressive mouthpiece then, serving a dual theatrical function. Like the first stasimon, the second ironically (and unintentionally) identifies Oedipus with Laius' killer; its concern with the purity of divine laws is an implicit contrast to the violations perpetrated by Oedipus. And the repetition of birth and begetting motifs drive this home, although the elders seem to be unaware of the deeper meaning of their words.

Third Stasimon

The third stasimon (or fourth ode) is typically Sophoclean, sometimes designated as one of his "cheerful odes," and it reflects Oedipus' new knowledge that he is not the child of Polybus and Merope, but a foundling. This giddy, deluded optimism intensifies the terrible reversal to come. Sophocles had the chorus of *Ajax* perform a similar song and dance, mistaking the hero's intentions, right before his suicide. The chorus of *Women of Trachis* ecstatically and ironically imagines Heracles burning with desire for Deianeira as he dons her fatal robe. Correspondingly the Theban elders excitedly speculate that their king might be the child of a god; for a brief moment anything is possible. Segal finds significance in the absence of Zeus in this song, the only choral ode without any reference to the god. Instead of the earlier theology espousing the purity of divine laws given birth in the aether, it imagines lustful gods cavorting in the human realm. The chorus describes itself speculatively as *mantis*, "prophet," reaffirming their belief in prophecy, but dangerously challenging their previous doubts about its accuracy. And these speculations are presented as an oath. Earlier they had sworn ignorance of Laius' killer, an oath very much like one from a court of law. And they were dismayed when their king refused to accept Creon's oath of denial. Now they affirm "by Olympus" their supposedly mantic speculations. They could not be further from the truth. The song is a trenchant demonstration of the fallibility of human understanding. But its form, invigorated by dance (indicated by the meter of the song), also suggests cultic associations with Dionysus (Henrichs 1994: 60). It simultaneously displays a self-awareness of the chorus' performance, similar to that of the preceding stasimon, albeit only hypothetical: the chorus predicts (as *mantis*) dancing on Mount Cithaeron in remembrance of its role as nurse of Oedipus and in honor of Apollo at the festival of the full moon (1086–97).

But the third stasimon, despite its optimism, is also on closer inspection bitingly ironic. Sansone (1975: 112) points out that it "parades before us the clues, the scattered pieces of the puzzle, that have accumulated throughout the play." The themes of the birth of laws and tyranny from previous songs are echoed in speculations about the birth of Oedipus. Earlier the chorus had declared that "*Hubris* begets the tyrant"; now it specifically denotes Oedipus as *tyrannos* (1095). While they had previously despaired that if prophecies were untrue, then they could no longer partake of the ritual dance, now they replace those prophecies with their own wild fantasies and look forward to a different ritual dance.

Fourth Stasimon

After the dramatic *anagnorisis* and *peripeteia* of the fourth episode the chorus confronts the terrible reality of their esteemed monarch's crimes and fallibilities. The disconnected metrical structure of the ode is an anomaly in a song cycle that exhibited balanced lyrical and thematic structure. The previous odes reflect the elders' belief in a knowable universe of divinely authored laws; their final discombobulated meters convey their understanding of the unknowable plight of all human beings; Oedipus is a model for the possibility of happiness for all mortals, including themselves, as the first stanza puts it.

The Second *Kommos*

The emotional register of the final moments of the tragedy is heightened by a *kommos* between Oedipus and the chorus in which they agree with his assessment of his life: it would be better had he never been born. Indeed they wish that they had never known him. The chorus, as so often, have the last words in the tragedy, seven lines addressed to the people of Thebes, in which they sum up the life of Oedipus, "who knew the famous riddle, and was a man most mighty" (1525), and ending with a general reflection: call no man blessed until he reaches the end of his life.

Analyzed as a series, this cycle of songs runs a gamut from profound religious wisdom, unconscious and ironic truth telling, metatheatric awareness of the chorus' ritual function, deluded optimism, and finally a tragic realization of the crimes of Oedipus, all held together by an interplay of different levels of narrative authority displaying the unique possibilities of choral polyphony. At times the elders are characters in the drama with inadequate understanding; at others they enunciate religious truths as if they are cultural voices; they express a self-referential awareness of their ritual performance; but they make ironic allusions to the crimes of Oedipus, as if they are conduits for a divine truth themselves. Tragedy offers rich possibilities for the manipulation of choral voice, as we saw in the last chapter, but in a play that thematizes the limitations of mortal knowledge, and the unseen forces operating on mortal lives, these different perspectives and levels of awareness are especially appropriate.

The Spectacle

One had only to hear the plot of a great tragedy to appreciate it, according to Aristotle. And while this is certainly true of Sophocles' *Oedipus*, the materiality of the drama contributes to its meaning—among the several reasons why this is the ancient tragedy staged most often in contemporary productions. The events of *Oedipus* occur at the intersection of different social spaces, public, private, ritual, and civic, existing in the material realm and yet often unseen, including the interior of the *skene*. While this particular *skene* could have been embellished with regal trappings, the most interesting aspect of Oedipus' royal residence, as the foregoing discussion emphasizes, is not its exterior features, but what happens within it, and relatedly what it signifies. The palace in the background is a private, domestic realm, and thus simultaneously a site of transgression (where Oedipus was born and also begot children with his mother), death (where Jocasta commits suicide), and self-mutilation (Oedipus' blinding). A great deal of important action occurs within its walls beyond the view of the audience, a phenomenon that resonates with the tragic limits of human knowledge thematized by the play.

Equally as significant is Oedipus' relationship to the *skene*. Using evidence from Aristophanes, Eric Csapo and William Slater (1994: 79–81) speculate that a stage joined to the orchestra by a series of steps was in use at least by the 420s; it would have been eminently suitable for Sophocles' *Oedipus*. In the prologue the king's position above the suppliants, and then the chorus, would convey an obvious message about his prestige. His position at the door of the palace is fixed; his centrality a sign of power, according to Donald Lateiner's analysis (2014: 1024) of the proxemics (human relationships to space) of the drama. But it could also be argued that his position in front of the *skene* is a sign of the constraints that bind him to his downfall and his complicated relationship to his household. This king never ventures into the stricken city, whose suffering is a consequence of his crime and whose altars are also laden with supplicatory offerings, nor does he travel to any of the locales, Mount Cithaeron, Corinth, or Delphi, that shaped his life. He sends or summons other people to and from these places, but when he leaves it is only to return within. Even at the end of the play, he does not immediately go into exile, in accordance with his own edict, but returns inside. His occupation of this interstitial zone, between the public world beyond and the private sphere within, is unusual for a male character. Tragic females, including Jocasta, and also Sophocles' Electra and Deianeira, are likewise closely bound to the domestic space and take up positions before the doorway. Oedipus is a unique individual whose personal life is intimately connected with his public role. His movements, closely circumscribed over the course of the drama, are a palpable signifier of how boxed in by his past actions he has become. His position between the public and private spheres is matched by a blurring of these two categories. Even though Creon, in the prologue, suggests moving inside to deliver his report from Delphi, Oedipus, in an apparent act of democratic openness, insists on sharing the news with the suppliants.

In addition to the architecture of the theater, the *skene*, and its peripheral spaces, there are two other material considerations, objects and bodies, both layered with dramatic and cultural meaning, which energize the performance space. It is evident from the opening lines of the play that altars are set before the *skene*. Although the suppliants depart at the end of the prologue, they leave behind their boughs wreathed with raw wool, a constant reminder of their suffering throughout the play. One of these altars belongs to Apollo, although the text does not specify this until Jocasta performs a second supplication. Her appeal gives important information about the space: "You are closest" (919), she says to the god, as she lays her offerings, which also remain visible for the rest of the play, on the symbol of his presence. His distinctive altar, identifiable by a shortened Ionic column, or his statue, has quietly emphasized that presence from the first moments.[14] In his study of the role of this god in the tragedy Drew Griffith (1996: 4) writes:

> Apollo is thoroughly present, in the sense that part of the architectural space of the theatre is demarcated as his precinct. This architectural device is exploited in the

stagecraft of the play to create the impression of Apollo's presence.

Apollo communicates to Laius, Oedipus, and the citizens of Thebes by means of his oracle at Delphi, and he remains throughout the tragedy in the realm of its "dark matter." In the early moments of the drama he has revealed that a polluted murderer dwells among the Thebans; and as the audience knows, that is Oedipus. The king's very physical presence is a source of pollution. It causes Tiresias to recoil from Oedipus, who demands to know why (386). Physical contact between characters is a marked and nuanced occurrence in all tragedy (discussed in detail by Maarit Kaimio 1988), but in this case it would carry a greater significance than usual. The chorus of elders, once it realizes who their king really is, also draws back from the *miastor* when he emerges from the *skene*. Judging from the text, the only people whom Oedipus touches are his daughters at the end of the play, children whose destinies have been shaped by their father's crimes.

It is not only other people who might be contaminated by his touch, but also objects. As suggested above, Oedipus probably held a scepter as a symbol of his authority. It is tempting to think of this implement as the very scepter with which he killed Laius. It too is saturated with its owner's pollution. The Athenians had a special court to try objects involved in accidental killings, which were tainted by miasma. By extension we can assume that this particular object, wielded by Oedipus, is analogously infected. But that scepter gains an added layer of meaning in the final scene: Tiresias had predicted that Oedipus would, by the end of the day, be guided like a blind man with his scepter. That is certainly how he makes his final entrance and departure.

Other aspects of performance lost to us include the actors' gestures, another aspect of their embodiment. The Greeks, like most cultures, had a rich repertoire of gestures, although again we are hampered by a lack of stage directions; vase paintings, however, give a sense of the range of non-verbal

communication (see especially Boegehold 1999). One valuable
source relevant to our play is a vase painted around 330 BCE,
about hundred years (Figure 6) after the first production of
Sophocles' *Oedipus*, although no figures are named. The
vessel, made in Sicily, probably depicts a Syracusan production.
Most scholars agree that it represents the critical moment in
the third episode when the Corinthian messenger reveals that
Oedipus is not the child of Polybus and Merope (Green 1994:
60, fig. 3.6; Taplin 2007, as item 22). Dramaturgy had evolved
and acting had become more professionalized, to be sure,
over that century, and fourth-century Sicilian conventions
were not necessarily identical with Athenian. An important
artifact nonetheless, it is one of only two depictions of a scene
from tragedy that unambiguously represent it as a dramatic
production, rather than a scene that dissolves the dramatic
space. The vase depicts a raised stage, supported by a series of
posts, and four columns representing the *skene*. Theaters had
undergone architectural changes by this time, and it is unlikely
that Sophocles' Athenian audiences would have seen this
architecture. But aspects of the painting preserve elements of
the production that must have been familiar to a fifth-century
audience. Two gestures provide some idea of ancient acting
style: Green (1996: 60–1) identifies the messenger's "speaking
gesture" (also visible on other vases that show messengers), an
extended hand with raised fingers. The other gesture is that
of Jocasta, who pulls her veil over her face, a signifier of her
distress, obviously at the precise moment of her recognition
of the truth of Oedipus' identity. It was up to the producer of
a play, and the individual actor, to decide how to express her
horror, but this gesture is ancient, described for example by
Homer, and it would have been a natural, easily recognizable
way to express intense emotion.

Two children appear with the adults on stage; there is
uncertainty about their identity, but they probably represent
Antigone and Ismene (who appear later in the play). They are
not masked, which was conventional for children in tragedy
(Green 1994: 61). There is nothing in the text to indicate

Figure 6 *Fragment of calyx krater (c. 330–320 BCE) with a scene from* Oedipus. *Courtesy Parco archeologico e paesaggistico di Siracusa, Paoli Orsi 66557*

their presence in the third episode, but there must have been mute characters, representing guards, servants, and the like in performance spaces, who were not acknowledged. We considered the possibility of mute characters in the prologue and second episode of Aeschylus' *Seven Against Thebes*, and it is equally as likely that Sophocles used mute actors. Jocasta, for example, had given an order to a servant earlier to bring Oedipus outside. The presence of these children, the product of Jocasta's incest, adds to the pathos and horror of the moment.

Audiences Past and Present

This original audience of Sophocles' tragedy had a special connection to the drama. On the one hand they could, to a certain extent, see their own city-state in Oedipus' Thebes, although, as Froma Zeitlin (1990: 131) has famously argued, Thebes functions in tragedy as "the negative model to Athens' manifest image of itself with regard to its notions of the proper management of city, society, and self." Over thirty known tragedies (most only survive as titles or fragments) were set in Thebes: their themes included incest, parricide, fratricide, civil war, improper burial, and other violations of the norms of civilized society. The Athenians, who believed their *polis* represented the pinnacle of civilization, observed a mythologized version of their sometimes enemy, not only to pat themselves on the back for not being Thebes, but also to negotiate their own unease about family and citizenship displaced onto this "anti-Athens." As this chapter has argued, they would recognize elements of their own homicide law, although not in a democratic context.

Sophocles' *Oedipus* is one of several tragedies featuring legal themes, which held a particular relevance for his original audience: the trial of Orestes for killing his mother in Aeschylus' *Eumenides* set in Athens and a different version for the same crime set in the city of Argos in Euripides' *Orestes* ask crucial questions about the administration of justice. These fictional trials resonated with the legal sensibilities of the citizens of Athens, who were not only notoriously litigious, but also had a keen interest in court proceedings. We hear of rowdy crowds watching trials in the *dikasteria* or "popular courts." The male citizens of Athens had a unique legal expertise: all were eligible (after the age of thirty) to serve on the massive juries that passed verdicts on an assortment of cases from assault to inheritance disputes. And since these same citizens were part of the audience of Sophocles' *Oedipus*, there can be little doubt that they recognized some of the procedures from their own homicide law, as this chapter has argued.

Although homicide trials were not held in these popular courts, an audience of legal experts would be watching Oedipus' investigation with intense interest. And it is quite possible that individual spectators passed different judgments on the guilt of Oedipus, just as two contemporary scholars have. One theory is that the audience would have found him guilty of "intentional homicide" (Harris 2010); the other theory is that since he was assaulted first by the cortege driver, and then Laius, he would only be guilty of "unintentional homicide" (Sommerstein 2011), since he was defending himself. Either way Oedipus was polluted, but in the latter scenario his punishment would be exile. Given the specific references to Draconian homicide law in the play, it is not hard to imagine the audience taking on the role of a jury. But of course this raises another question: was the intended audience of tragedy male citizens of Athens, either in the theater of Dionysus or one of the Attic deme theaters?

To a certain extent it was, but as the aforementioned Sicilian vase attests Sophocles' *Oedipus* had a far-ranging appeal in the ancient world. Moreover its themes of knowledge and human agency are relevant in many ways to diverse audiences, including those in more recent times. The civic, and hence democratic, inflection of tragedy is a topic hotly debated by scholars (summarized and assessed by Henderson 2007: 179–95). But the ancient audiences of tragedies included foreigners, metics (resident aliens), members of different social classes, and probably women (Roselli 2011: 125). The next chapter will speculate about the reception of female audience members in antiquity and also consider the production of tragedy throughout the Mediterranean world. But no discussion of this famous play would be complete without acknowledging how it continues to have relevance for more recent audiences. Sophocles' *Oedipus* has been performed countless times since its first revival in the nineteenth century. Peter Arnott's marionette production, which toured North America in 1986, conveyed the sense that its characters were ultimately controlled by a master puppeteer, always visible above the action. The 1997 masked production, *Oedipus Rex*, in Stratford, Ontario, used a thrust stage and theater in the round, bringing the audience closer to the spectacle. The director of this version was Douglas Campbell, who had played the role of Oedipus in an identical 1955 production and whose son Benedict Campbell now took the role of Oedipus. At the other end of the spectrum is Pan Pan Theater's 2006 production in Dublin, *Oedipus Loves You*, a Rock Opera mash-up of Sophocles' *Oedipus* and *Antigone*, with abundant Freudian references for good measure: the production opened with a naked Tiresias, in high heeled pumps, playing guitar, to the discomfiture of spectators in the front row. In 2005, the small Arcola Theater in London produced Ola Rotimi's 1961 adaptation, *The Gods Are Not to Blame*, set in the Yoruba Kingdom of Africa. The audience sat in a circle around the performers, thus becoming absorbed in the action of the drama, perhaps like audiences in ancient Athens.

But the tragedy's concern with contagion and community took on new significance during the early months of the COVID-19 pandemic when Theater of War Productions offered *The Oedipus Project*, a dramatic reading of Sophocles' *Oedipus*, using the virtual meeting platform Zoom (May 7, 2020). Over 15,000 viewers throughout the world watched the production using a technology that became a household word during the pandemic. The cast included Oscar Isaac as Oedipus, Frances McDormand as Jocasta, John Turturro as Creon, and New York City Public Advocate Jumaane Williams as the chorus. Krishni Burns (2020) reports that Issac "was adept at making Sophocles' translated text sound like something a contemporary person might say over Zoom, and he used the camera expertly to enhance his characterization. His Oedipus was every inch the modern media-savvy politician." Every age, it seems, gets the *Oedipus* it needs.

4

Innovation: Euripides' *Helen*

Euripides, youngest of the three canonical tragedians and arguably the most controversial in his day, died in 406 BCE, only months before Sophocles, whose *Oedipus at Colonus* (produced posthumously in 401) has the distinction of being the last surviving specimen of its genre. Although OC marks the end of his sixty-five-year career, Sophocles employs a traditional form: the wandering exile Oedipus arrives in Athens with his daughters as a suppliant to spend his last moments; he encounters a sympathetic chorus of elders, whose odes divide the drama into episodes; three actors play characters that include Oedipus' family, Theseus, and a messenger who recounts his apotheosis in a sacred grove represented by the *skene*. The basic structure of tragedy was much the same as it had been when Sophocles produced his Oedipus three decades earlier. From the mid-fifth century on production became more professionalized with prizes awarded to actors, but when Euripides made his debut in 455 there had been no major innovations in tragic dramaturgy for over a decade, nor would there be any to come: the number of speaking actors was fixed at three; the chorus was still fifteen members, and although their odes are shorter, it is still a vital presence in the drama; the architecture of the theater, to the best of our knowledge, remained the same. There is evidence to suggest that the costumes of actors and choruses evolved over the century, becoming more fitted to the body, with ornately patterned fabrics in some cases, as exemplified by the tragic actor depicted on the Pronomos Vase (*c.* 400 BCE, Figure 7), but very little is known about changes in the use of props or

Figure 7 *Detail from the Pronomos Vase. Courtesy Getty Museum*

scenic decoration. Wyles (2011: 20–33), synthesizing visual representations (ceramic vase paintings and a relief sculpture), comments on the variation of costumes and tentatively suggests "a hint of a more stable form" at the end of the fifth century.

Of course, it is unscientific to make pronouncements based on 3 percent of tragedies produced in the fifth century, but even this small sample attests to the versatility of a genre that still retained a consistent formal structure. Although he inherited and maintained a well-established form, Euripides reveals tragedy's capacity for innovation with his iconoclastic treatment of myth, psychological realism (especially of female characters), details of everyday life, and innovations in music and dance, collectively known as *choreia*.

More of Euripides' work than of the other two tragedians combined comes down to us, thanks to a manuscript containing nine of his plays in alphabetical order, in addition to ten other dramas preserved separately. He was granted a chorus, according to the most reliable ancient sources, for twenty-two tetralogies (eighty-eight dramas in total) in his career (455 to 405 BCE), but placed first only four times, in contrast to Aeschylus' thirteen victories and Sophocles' eighteen. It bears remembering that the tetralogy containing Sophocles' *Oedipus Tyrannus* did not place first at the City Dionysia, for reasons we can only guess. A more important index of success is that state officials saw fit to grant Euripides an entry in the dramatic festivals so often. His extant tragedies along with substantial fragments, while less than a quarter of his total output, shed light on the development of his artistry and the elasticity of the genre.[1] The surviving plays (dating from *Alcestis* in 438 BCE) afford a sense of how he exploited the formulaic structures at his disposal in his distinctive style. Furthermore, critiques and citations by his contemporaries—he is the playwright cited most often by Aristotle, and Aristophanes takes any opportunity to parody him—are insights, albeit limited and exaggerated, into how ancient audiences responded to his work.[2] By the fourth century BCE he was the most popular of the Greek tragedians at home and abroad; his dramas continue to resonate in our own time. Euripides is capable of creating intense pity and fear, those essential ingredients of catharsis identified by Aristotle. His *Medea*, who agonizes over whether to kill her two young sons, a crime that Euripides probably invented for her, epitomizes the emotional gravity that he is capable of generating.

Medea (431 BCE) is one of his earliest surviving plays, but we encounter the same tragic profundity in later work. His final quartet, including *Iphigenia at Aulis*, which survives, and *Alcmaeon in Corinth*, which does not, was awarded first prize and produced posthumously by a relative (*c.* 405). It also included his *Bacchae*, which presents the god of theater himself, Dionysus, exacting revenge on his recalcitrant mortal cousin, Pentheus, for resisting his worship. The young king of Thebes is mercilessly destroyed by dismemberment and beheading at the hands of frenzied maenads including his own mother, who, under the god's influence, mistake him for a wild animal. The tragedy has an archaic feel about it; the simple revenge plot leads to catastrophe. The chorus, representing foreign maenads, performs five odes, breaking the drama into the formulaic prologue, episodes, and exodus; they act in the conventional capacity of witnesses to the action, although their delight at the terrible fate of Pentheus and his mother adds a horrific timbre to the final moments. They are among the few choruses who are not members of the protagonist's community, or marginalized females, but we have only to look back to the chorus of Furies in Aeschylus' *Eumenides* half a century earlier to recognize that they are not unique.

While *Bacchae* instantiates a tragic reversal from good fortune to bad, a *peripeteia* can also be from a bad situation to a happy one, as Aristotle recognized and Sophocles' *Oedipus at Colonus* exemplifies. This chapter scrutinizes such a play, *Helen* (412 BCE), produced in the declining years of the Athenian empire, a drama that showcases how adeptly Euripides could manipulate the genre or, more precisely, how the genre could accommodate a range of different tones. Although it is difficult to generalize about late tragedy, it does seem that innovation was in the air in the last decades of the century. Plays such as Euripides' *Orestes*, which adds an entire episode to the period between Orestes' matricide and his trial in Athens, as dramatized by Aeschylus (an innovation in itself), introduces startling revisions of the canonical myth, including the murder of Helen, and the abduction of her daughter Hermione, and such novelties as a singing eunuch. Euripides knew his audience well; it became one of his most popular plays. The celebrated tragedian Agathon, whose work survives only as a few fragments and titles, may have followed Euripides' lead (or vice versa) with experimentation in myth-based plots; he went one step further with his *Antheus*, a tragedy based on no traditional narrative (Aristotle *Poet.* 1451b). Agathon's career in Athens was short, perhaps less than a decade, but he was evidently highly regarded. Wright (2016: 59–90) examines testimonia for his life and career and contemplates the possibility that Agathon made radical changes to myths. The setting for Plato's *Symposium* is a party in honor of one of his victories. Aristophanes, also in attendance at the event, considered Agathon's music sufficiently avant-garde to mock in the prologue of his *Thesmophoriazusai* (411 BCE), although that comedy is otherwise devoted to a hilarious parody of Euripides' *Helen* and *Andromeda*, produced the preceding year.

Helen is exemplary for its inventive use of music, reworking of mythical material, redoubtable heroine, complex plot, and masterful disruption of dramaturgical convention. Making its debut in 412 at the City Dionysia, it typifies a group of Euripidean plays dominated by likeable and successful female characters. *Helen* dramatizes an alternate version of the famous myth: Hera has fashioned a simulacrum of the most beautiful woman alive, which Paris has taken to Troy, while the god Hermes takes the real Helen to Egypt to be protected by the good King Proteus. When the play opens, Proteus is recently deceased; his son Theoclymenus is pressuring Helen to marry him. Returning from the war, Menelaus is shipwrecked in Egypt with the phantom, or *eidolon*, which vanishes when he encounters his wife. The couple is happily reunited, and with the support of Proteus' daughter, the prophetic Theonoe, they devise a ruse that allows them to escape by a ship unsuspectingly provided by Theoclymenus. The tetralogy included *Andromeda*, several hundred lines of which survive, set in Ethiopia and treating the rescue of the captive princess by Perseus; there is no reliable evidence for the third tragedy or for the satyr drama. Wright (2005: 44–9), who rejects arguments for dating *Iphigenia in Tauris* earlier than *Helen*, argues that it was the third tragedy in the tetralogy. Structurally it is very similar to *Helen*; its plot met with Aristotle's approval for a simultaneous recognition and reversal. Iphigenia, rescued from her father's sacrificial knife just before the Trojan War, is spirited away to Tauris (now Crimea), where she presides as a priestess of Artemis over a cult of human sacrifice. She recognizes her brother Orestes, slated for immolation, just in time, orchestrates a plan to deceive the barbarian king Thoas, and the siblings sail home. Many of these elements, including the recognition and reunion of family members, tricking a foreign king, and escaping by ship, occur in *Helen*, which bolsters Wright's argument. But most scholars (including Allan, in his 2008 edition and commentary) reject the possibility, based on stylistic features including variations in meter. C. W. Marshall (2014), in his study of the stagecraft of *Helen*, suggests that *IT* was produced several years earlier as part of a cluster of experimental tragedies that includes *Ion*, another play featuring a happy reversal. The following discussion will consider several similarities in all three plays, but this does not assume (or reject) that they were part of the same package. All feature noble female characters, Helen, Iphigenia, and Creusa, whose unhappy situations are overturned when they reunite with a lost family member—husband, brother, or son. These three plays also exhibit an interest in women's ritual lives, including an influential priestess, a topic considered toward the end of this chapter.

The previous chapter surveyed Sophocles' *Oedipus Tyrannus* as a paradigm of mature tragedy by considering the intertwining of characterization and plot, the role of the chorus, physical elements and dramatic space, and audience. Euripides' *Helen* offers a different way of analyzing the same components, including formulaic scenes, and other stock elements, because it often provocatively stretches the limits of those elements. Confronted with what often seem to be humorous moments, and a romantic ending, contemporary scholarship has tried to pigeonhole the play into contemporary generic categories. There are amusing elements, to be sure, deriving from the deflated heroic masculinity of the shipwrecked Menelaus or Helen's skillful deception of the ardent barbarian king Theoclymenus. The subsequent joyful reunions of male and female family members are distinctly similar to plots of New Comedy produced in Athens during the next century, and in Rome a few centuries later, from which Shakespeare's comedies are descended. Desmond Conacher (1967) writes of "melodrama," and Anne Burnett (1971) describes the play as "romantic comedy." As Wright points out, ancient audiences did not use these categories. Aristotle considers *Iphigenia in Tauris*, which Helen resembles in its plot, as a tragedy, and he gives no consideration to any genre other than tragedy, comedy, and satyr drama.[3] Marshall argues that Euripides is drawing on Aeschylus' *Proteus*, the lost satyr drama of the *Oresteia*, but *Helen* is still indisputably tragic in terms of its structure and because it was produced at the competition for tragedy at the City Dionysia.

Before proceeding to an analysis of the play, we should briefly acknowledge the historical moment in which *Helen* was produced. This was an uneasy period, as Athens, ravaged by the Peloponnesian War, lurched toward capitulation to Sparta at the end of the century. In 415 the Athenian democratic assembly, under the influence of the popular politician Alcibiades, had voted for a naval invasion of Sicily in the hope of acquiring resources to continue the war. In an effort to squelch the expedition the well-respected general Nicias demanded an exorbitant amount of ships and resources to complete the mission. Contrary to his expectation, the democratic assembly approved the request. By 413, the year before *Helen* was produced, it was evident that the Athenian expedition was a disaster, with the fleet destroyed, and thousands of men killed or imprisoned. The troops that did manage to escape returned home deeply traumatized. To what extent these events shaped an audience's experience of *Helen* is impossible to determine, and of course each spectator brought a different set of values and experience to the theater. Nonetheless with thousands of casualties, there were few Athenians who did not feel the impact of the catastrophe in some way. While it might be tempting to read a play about a war fought for a phantom as a comment on the delusions informing the Sicilian expedition, it is important to acknowledge that Athenian democracy continued to vote for war in the decade that followed. And besides Euripides does not present the Trojan War as futile: as Helen explains in her opening monologue (39), it was part of Zeus's plan to reduce the population of the earth and enhance the glory of Achilles.

In Homer's *Odyssey* Helen drugs her audience in Sparta when she tells her story of the Trojan War. Is Euripides' *Helen*, with its fairytale setting and comic moments, analogously a balm for the wounded psyche of Athens? Such an argument would need to account for the vicious battle fought on board the escape ship, described by an eyewitness toward the end of the play, during which Helen bloodthirstily urges on the Greeks as they slaughter the Egyptian crew. Despite her chaste absence from Troy, she manages to reinscribe herself in the text as the instigator of war. These final moments belie the interpretation of the text as a light-hearted confection or escapist fantasy, as some earlier critics maintained (for example A. M. Dale's 1967 commentary on the play).

We miss much of the play's meaning if we read it as an antiwar tract, an oblique salvo at Athenian foreign policy, or a palliative diversion. A more sophisticated approach to *Helen*'s reception takes its intellectual context into account. Peter Burian's fine discussion (2007: 25) connects its dialectic of reality and illusion with the theme of purity and guilt throughout the drama. Mark Ringer (2016: 235) describes it as Euripides' "most overtly philosophical play" and argues that the playwright, throughout his career, displays an erudite engagement with the intellectual trends of his time. Beneath *Helen*'s playful surface lies a subtle philosophical meditation informed by the cutting-edge discourse of contemporary Greek thinkers. A dominant theme is the antithesis between reality and appearance, embodied respectively by the real Helen in Egypt, and her replacement phantom in Troy, "an empty fantasy (*dokēsin*)," which Paris only "seems (*dokei*) to have" (35–6), a delusion that accentuates the limits and fallibility of human knowledge. An epistemological frailty is at the core of Sophocles' *Oedipus*, as the previous chapter noted, but Euripides is more attuned to the philosophical trends of the late fifth century in his approach. The play's dualities suggest the influence of Sophism, an intellectual movement represented by figures such as Protagoras, Gorgias, and Antiphon. Although much maligned as an avaricious and destructive element by conservative critics, Sophism was in fact a vigorous and varied form of philosophy, concerned with rhetoric, moral values, and social theories. The movement's influence on Euripides is by no means limited to *Helen*, as Conacher (1998) and others have elucidated, but the play's focus on delusion and the limitations of sensory perception, topics of Sophistic inquiry, is particularly acute and handled with considerable flair.[4] These ideas also anticipate Plato's dichotomies between appearance and a deeper sense of reality, articulated for example in his *Republic*. Noting that Plato would have been about sixteen when *Helen* was produced, Segal (1971: 257) speculates that he could have been in its audience.

Helen's antitheses are congruent with its self-reflexive allusions to artistic production, which begin in the prologue. Teucer, a survivor of the Trojan War, who makes a brief stop in Egypt, cannot believe his eyes when he encounters Helen:

> O gods, what a sight do I see here! I behold the deadly, hateful image (likeness) of Helen, who destroyed me, and all the Achaeans. May the gods cast you out, such an imitation (*mimema*) of Helen as you are. (74–7)[5]

The ancient audience of course is looking at a *mimema* of Helen, a male actor wearing a mask. When that actor goes inside the *skene* later in the play to change from white to black garments and a different mask, returning as Helen in the role of grieving widow, he draws attention to the function of the building where actors change costumes and emerge as different characters. Relatedly, costume accentuates the character of Menelaus, who is defined to a significant degree by his clothing or lack thereof. When he arrives in the acting space after surviving a shipwreck, he is clad only in the tattered remnants of sailcloth.[6] Even though Helen has been advised that her husband will soon land in Egypt, she does not recognize him when he appears, because he is wearing a "wretched garment." And this sentiment is echoed by Theoclymenus (1204), which allows Menelaus to remain undetected. His pathetic rags match his futile attempts to summon his former martial glory at Troy, which proves useless in the alternate reality of Egypt. Only when he is re-costumed, wearing the garb suited to his status, is he able to take more control of the situation, although paradoxically he is playing the role of the messenger of his own death.[7] By drawing attention to its own status as a fiction and the ability of costume to disguise a character's identity and intentions, *Helen* incorporates and animates the precepts of Sophism in a display of metatheater, thereby inviting its audiences to meditate on the nature of reality, how we perceive it, and the limitations of our senses.

The drama is a concoction of surprises and novelties, among which are its four major characters. Two are radically altered from conventional depiction. The chaste and noble Helen, her reputation sullied by reports of adultery, is more typically represented in Euripides' *Trojan Women* (415 BCE) as entitled, manipulative, and destructive. Her rather dim-witted husband, Menelaus, with his conspicuously inappropriate recourse to modes of interaction that recall Homeric epics, behaves as if still on the battlefield in a situation that requires diplomacy and subtlety. The other duo is entirely of Euripides' invention: the Egyptian royal siblings, Theonoe, a priestess-seer of rare cosmic affinities, and the young king Theoclymenus, Helen's unwanted suitor. The plot likewise deviates from tradition. Although there were accounts by the sixth-century epic poet Steisichorus and the fifth-century historian Herodotus that Helen did not go to Troy, Euripides has expanded the alternative version with his own embellishments and yet ultimately circles back to the same conclusion as the received tradition: Helen and Menelaus return to Sparta (Dunn 1995: 152; Allan 2008: 18–28).

The spirit of novelty and innovation extends as well to *Helen*'s use of formulaic scenes and structures, which can be combined, disrupted, or destabilized to create new meanings. This chapter approaches the play in terms of the conventions that it manipulates and, in so doing, explores those conventions in depth. We begin with an overview of an influential analysis that identifies the drama's structure based on a mythic story pattern of rebirth and return. From there we parse different elements of plot and character to see how Euripides has used the building blocks of tragic drama, for example type scenes, in unexpected ways to produce suspense and excitement. The songs and unusual role of the chorus are considered next. As previous chapters observed, the physical and material elements of production are integral to its meaning, and as we shall see, this is no less true for *Helen*. The chapter concludes by considering alternative audiences of the play, i.e., the reception of female spectators and non-Athenian audiences in reproductions of the play in foreign venues.

The Myth of Rebirth and Return

It is widely acknowledged that *Helen* combines two complementary story patterns: the abduction of Persephone by Hades, best known from the sixth-century epic poem *The Homeric Hymn to Demeter*, and the reunion of Penelope and Odysseus from the *Odyssey* (see, for example, Segal 1971: 569–73; Foley 2001: 303–31). The first of these intertexts may derive from Helen's role as a Spartan goddess of vegetation, who died and was reborn cyclically like Persephone (Zweig 1999). In Euripides, Helen's tale conforms to a narrative pattern of virgins being abducted while picking flowers (Wolff 1973: 63–4). Of course Helen is no maiden, but there need not be an exact parallel for the correspondence, since other allusions to the Persephone myth strengthen the comparison (Allan 2008: 178).

In her study of the roles of women in Greek tragedy, Helene Foley (2001) groups *Helen* with the earlier *Alcestis* in the category of *anodos* ("ascent") drama, based on the myth of Persephone's abduction by Hades, and temporary return to the land of the living and her mother Demeter. An *anodos* drama capitalizes on the myth's conflation of marriage and death and the social meaning of marriage as the symbolic death of one identity and rebirth as another, a common juxtaposition in tragedy (Rehm 1994). The conflation manifests, for example, when Alcestis, who volunteered to die in place of her husband, is restored to life at the end of her name-play in a scene that recalls a Greek wedding. The Persephone analogy is more explicit in *Helen*, however. Although Helen, like Alcestis, is a married woman, and an exemplary one at that, her account of abduction by Hermes while she was picking flowers bears more specific similarities with the abduction of the virginal Persephone by Hades.[8] The focus in the prologue is the tomb of Proteus, king of Egypt, a country whose wealth and famous funerary cults help to construe it as a version of the underworld. Helen's opening words, an invocation of the "lovely maiden (*kalliparthenoi*) streams of the Nile" (1), establish the theme of purity and virginity, which reverberates throughout the play and enhances her association with Persephone. The choral odes, discussed in more detail below, expand upon the theme and specifically reference the myth of the distraught mother goddess.

Helen is able to restore her previous identity as the wife of Menelaus, and her unblemished reputation, by staging a false funeral for her husband; she dons mourning garb and cuts her hair to deceive Theoclymenus into believing that Menelaus is dead and that she is preparing to marry the Egyptian king. As Foley suggests (2001: 312), her appearance would evoke the Spartan custom of brides cutting their hair for their marriage ceremony as described by Plutarch (*Lycurgus* 15.3–5). Marriage and death thus become intermingled concepts, as they are in the myth of Persephone. The return of Helen to Sparta with Menelaus is accordingly analogous to Persephone's return to Demeter. Foley argues that the ascent of Persephone provides an analogy for the experiences of Euripides' female characters that allows him to imbue them with glory and renown, a delicate maneuver in a culture that valued female modesty and social invisibility. Like Persephone, Helen and Alcestis obtain cultic honors after their ordeals. Their rewards and visibility do not threaten the stability of the patriarchal order but rather affirm it. Euripides uses the stereotype of the duplicitous woman, but Helen can be heroic rather than dangerous if she deploys that characteristic in the service of her marriage to Menelaus (Holmberg 1995: 37–8). Her reputation is thus rehabilitated and she returns to Sparta as the chaste wife of Menelaus. The Persephone analogy is strengthened by the knowledge that Helen was worshipped as a goddess in Spartan cults, a status foreshadowed by choral songs, and secured by the divine intervention of her brothers at the end of the drama.

Reunion of separated family members, at the heart of the Persephone myth, is also the narrative destination of Homer's *Odyssey*, which *Helen* also recalls. Homer's epic includes an episode in which Menelaus encounters Proteus, a sea god not a king, off the coast of Egypt (4.351–592), and alludes to Helen and Menelaus spending time in Egypt on the way home from Troy (4.125–230). While these references might be the inspiration for the Egyptian setting, the representation of Helen as a loyal wife resisting another marriage is an obvious echo of faithful Penelope. And the delayed recognition of her husband, washed ashore and seemingly destitute, casts Menelaus in the role of Odysseus.

This strategy of allusion is related to the self-reflexivity of tragedy discernible in all three surviving authors, but especially pronounced in Euripides. On the one hand, *Helen*'s self-conscious acknowledgment of illusion is consonant with Sophistic dichotomies of appearance and reality, but by suggestively questioning the legitimacy of mythology and provocatively replacing a tale of adultery and betrayal with allusions to traditional tales of wholesome marriage and sexual purity, the play draws attention to its own status as fiction in a display of what Isabelle Torrance (2013) identifies as Euripidean "metapoetry." Moreover, what Euripides does on a macro-level, i.e., subverting, eliding, and distorting well-known traditional tales, he also does in terms of smaller units of plot structure and formal elements of tragedy, to which we now turn.

Structure and Themes

Prologue

In contrast to the spareness of Aeschylus' *Seven*, or the elegant economy of Sophocles' *Oedipus*, there is a busy quality about Euripides' later tragedies (Dunn 2015); the complex plot of *Helen* is characteristic in this respect. The play begins with a suppliant tableau, a common scene in tragedy; as we have already seen, Sophocles' *Oedipus Tyrannus* opens with a group supplication. The convention goes back at least as far as Aeschylus' *Suppliant Women*, in which the chorus of Danaids petitions the Argive king for sanctuary from their pursuing Egyptian suitors. Euripides' *Andromache* opens with the captive widow of Hector, now the concubine of Achilles' son Neoptolemus, seeking protection from his wife Hermione; she is protected by the intervention of Achilles' father Peleus.[9] Helen is more mobile, assertive, and independent than other suppliant women and turns out to be perfectly capable of orchestrating her own salvation.

In other respects the prologue is typically Euripidean. It opens with a monologue, as do seven other Euripidean plays, in which Helen provides the necessary background to the ensuing drama. Hermes, she reveals, promised that she would return to Sparta with Menelaus, but within moments she encounters a survivor of the war, Teucer, who suggests otherwise. As he does in several other plays Euripides uses the prologue to introduce a prophecy and then teases the audience with the possibility that it will not be fulfilled.[10] Thus begins a play that trades on inconsistencies and thwarted expectations (Boedeker 2017).

First Episode

The prologue ends with the arrival of the chorus, but the chorus' function as a structural marker of the divisions of tragedy is henceforth contorted. The complex first episode is stretched to an unusual length by the delayed first stasimon. The following discussion follows Burian (2007) in marking the end of the first episode at the first stasimon, which is the convention. Allan (2008), however, prefers to divide the episode at the second entry of the chorus, when it sings a very short song. Regardless of how we label the division, the episode is highly unusual. Our analysis breaks the episode into interrelated parts with remarks about the conventional and innovative aspects of each.

After hearing of Teucer's news and the possibility of Menelaus' death, the chorus leader advises Helen to seek counsel from Theonoe to learn if her husband is still alive. And then follows a unique occurrence in extant tragedy: the chorus enters the *skene* with her. The women's remarkable departure effectively creates a second prologue when Menelaus, recently shipwrecked and clad in salvaged rags—hardly what Helen was expecting—enters an empty performance space. An exchange at the door of the palace with a female porter, who shoos him off with a warning of her dangerous king, is a touch of comedy after the preceding joint lamentation by Helen and the chorus. But there is also a pathetic quality to Menelaus' befuddlement as he tries to weigh the old woman's astounding assertion that Helen of Sparta lives within the palace against the evidence of his own senses that he left Troy with Helen. Confused, and stripped of the material emblems of his status, he ponders the ambiguity of names—people and places share names, but his own famous name is unknown in this exotic place. Shortly thereafter Helen and the chorus come out the same door.

Recognition and Reversal

All indications are that Helen and Menelaus will soon be in each other's arms, but Euripides prolongs this fulfillment with a recognition scene that is, even by his own standards, complex and full of action. According to Aristotle, as we saw in the previous chapter, the *anagnorisis* (recognition) is an important element of the tragic plot; Euripides is constantly reinventing this pivotal moment. His earliest surviving play *Alcestis* ends when Admetus recognizes the veiled woman before him as his wife, brought back from the dead by Heracles, but this is after he achieved a different kind of recognition, that his household was lost without her. In later plays Euripides offers ingenious variations on recognitions between long-lost family members that lead to happy reversals. The best preserved of his fragmentary tragedies, *Hypsipyle*, probably from the last decade of his career, treats the reunion of the enslaved queen of Lemnos, mother of Jason's sons, with her long-lost children. In *Ion*, mother and son have tried to kill each other, but recognizing a piece of weaving that swaddled the infant Ion, Creusa apprehends that Ion is her son, set out to die after birth. In *Bacchae*, a messenger reports the moment when Pentheus realizes the gravity of his repudiation of Dionysus. In the final moments of the play his mother, Agave, comes out of her delusion to understand that she is holding not the head of a lion, but that of Pentheus, a gruesome reworking of the convention.

Two other Euripidean plays, based on events after the murder of Agamemnon, explore the varied possibilities of a stylized moment whose origins are the recognition of Orestes by his sister Electra in Aeschylus' *Choephori*, thus framing a fictional *anagnorisis* with the audience's recognition of these prior texts. Euripides' *Electra* distorts the Aeschylean version of Orestes' recognition by his sister through the signs of a lock of hair, a footprint, and a scrap of cloth, all of which Electra scathingly rejects. Torrance (2013: 14–19, 28–30) offers a detailed analysis of the different components of the recognition tokens in Electra and suggests that Euripides is not so much making a target of Aeschylus, as the convention itself. And in *Iphigenia in Tauris*, Orestes realizes that the woman about to send him to the sacrificial altar is his sister when she produces a letter for her family in Argos. There are no physical tokens to prove his identity, but when he describes a piece of cloth that Iphigenia wove as a young girl (*IT* 817), he hits the mark. While these three plays depend to varying degrees on a familiarity with Aeschylus' prototype, the recognition of Menelaus by Helen is closer to the Odyssean paradigm: in his tattered clothing he corresponds to Odysseus disguised as a beggar before Penelope, who needs to recognize him in order to complete the story.

Each of Euripides' extant recognition scenes creates suspense in its own way, and it is possible to see a development despite the uncertainty of dating the plays precisely. In the earliest version *Electra* (produced between 420 and 415 BCE), Orestes visits his sister, married off to a lowly peasant, to enlist her aid, but does not reveal his identity in a prolonged dialogue in stichomythia. It is not until an old man, summoned to bring provisions for hospitality, recognizes Orestes and, by pointing to a scar on her brother's face, persuades Electra of his identity. The siblings' embrace is brief; twenty lines, including a short choral song, lead almost perfunctorily to the plot to kill their father's murderer, Aegisthus. In *Ion*, the recognition occurs while Creusa seeks asylum as a suppliant to avoid being charged with attempted murder and comes late in the play after a false recognition. Her husband Xuthus has received an oracle that Ion is *his* son, and the play ends with Creusa and Ion implicitly agreeing to let him continue the belief.

In *Electra* and *IT*, recognition precedes the intrigue that accomplishes a reversal, a pattern that also operates in *Helen*, but audience expectations are frustrated by disruptions and delays. The deferral of the recognition between Helen and Menelaus is made more natural by the unusual departure of the chorus, who are not on hand to witness his arrival. As Helen and the chorus emerge from the *skene*, their song reveals the welcome news that Theonoe was able to provide. Yet even though Helen now knows her husband will reach Egypt, the unkempt stranger lurking before the tomb, her place of refuge, is disquieting. She cannot see him for who he is, because of his "unsightly garment" (554), an inversion of the recognition by textile motif of Euripides' earlier plays. It is as if the drama is reverting to its suppliant play formula, with a woman in flight from a dangerous male, as Helen rushes to the tomb. But then the familiar pattern prevails. In keeping with Euripides' recognition sequences, there is a passage of stichomythia exchanged between long-lost relatives, but that leads only to Helen's frustration and the audience's disappointed expectations. She realizes that the man before her is Menelaus, but he cannot comprehend, despite her appearance and her report of the phantom Helen, that she is his wife. Only a messenger's announcement of the disappearance of the phantom, who obligingly validates Helen's version of events as it ascends back to the sky, can move the plot forward. And this is yet another variation of a common device—a *deus ex machina* of sorts, who prevents the plot from going off the rails. In contrast to the recognitions accomplished by Electra and Orestes, Iphigenia and Orestes, and Creusa and Ion, who piece together the truth through tokens, memory, and logic, Helen depends on the knowledge provided by Theonoe's contact with divine *aether*, and Menelaus is persuaded only by the message of the phantom as it ascends back to that same invisible substance.

The intense emotion of the recognition between husband and wife, separated for seventeen years, is conveyed by an ecstatic duet, reminiscent of a similar operatic reunion of Orestes and Iphigenia in *IT*, but missing from the earlier *Electra*. Most of the lyrics go to Helen, although Menelaus sings too; the closest comparison is with the reunion of Iphigenia, who sings, and Orestes, who responds in spoken words. The next stage in this sequence, as we would expect, is the development of an intrigue. In *Electra*, Orestes and his accomplices make plans to kill Aegisthus at sacrifice, while Electra will use a fictitious childbirth to lure Clytemnestra to her death. Correspondingly Iphigenia formulates a strategy to escape by ship from Tauris with Artemis' cult statue, which she pretends to take to the sea for a ritual bathing; Orestes' ship will be ready to set sail. In like manner, intrigue follows recognition for Helen and Menelaus, but complications create suspense despite the familiarity of the plot elements. Any action is forestalled by Helen's realization that the omniscient Theonoe could tell her brother of Menelaus' arrival. Menelaus' plan, in which Helen is willing to participate, is a suicide pact to prevent Theoclymenus from killing him and marrying Helen. But she has a better idea, which involves reverting to her initial supplicatory posture and appealing to Theonoe.

The Theonoe Scene

The Theonoe scene occurs at the midpoint in the drama, and when it is over, the fortunes of Helen and Menelaus have taken a turn for the better.[11] It deserves close scrutiny for several reasons, not the least because it exemplifies Euripides' penchant for formal structures, and correspondingly his variations of those structures, but also because it features a recurring figure in plays of this period, the virgin priestess. This otherwise unknown Egyptian seer, the reason for Teucer's visit, plays a critical role: first by assuring Helen that Menelaus is alive, and then, after participating in a divine tribunal, by helping to deceive her brother Theoclymenus. The insertion of the Theonoe scene is an unusual element in the recognition-deception sequence. If we compare the most similar plot structure, we note that *Iphigenia in Tauris* moves directly from recognition to plotting. The notional threat posed by Theonoe, expected to be loyal to her brother, adds an additional obstacle to overcome in *Helen*. Helen is well aware that any attempt to escape requires the support and cooperation of the seer, whom it would be impossible to deceive. That Theonoe appears immediately at the doorway to the palace at this moment is uncanny. More uncanny is her direct communication with the gods currently debating whether to let Helen leave with Menelaus, as Hera goddess of marriage wishes, or have her remain in Egypt, to satisfy the injured pride of Aphrodite, whose support of Paris was based on an illusion.

Theonoe's arrival at the door of the palace is marked by an exotic ceremony: one female attendant fumigates the air with sulphur; a second purifies the ground with a torch. In many respects, including her rigorous concern with purity, Theonoe is typical of the cluster of priestess characters in Euripidean drama, especially in his later period. These include Cassandra, Trojan seer and priestess of Apollo, who makes a brief appearance in *Trojan Women* (*c*. 415 BCE). A fragment from *Auge* (*c*. 410) features a priestess of Athena, apparently performing a cleansing ritual. Iphigenia performs purification rites early in *IT*. These ceremonies were common elements in Greek religion and could invite the spectators to think of the sacerdotal women so important for their own state religion. Another fragment, from the end of *Erechtheus*, an earlier play (*c*. 422), has Athena appointing Praxithea, an Athenian queen, as the first priestess of Athena Polias, the most important religious functionary in Athens, who might have been the template for the heroine of *Iphigenia in Tauris*. Thus Laura McClure (2016) reads Iphigenia as a version of the renowned Lysimache, a long-lived and well-respected priestess of Athena Polias, still alive in this final decade of Euripides' career. One speculation (Lewis 1955), supported by inscriptional evidence, is that the heroine of Aristophanes' *Lysistrata* (411 BCE), produced within a few years of *IT* and *Helen*, was modeled on Lysimache. Also notable is the Pythia, priestess of Apollo, who made an appearance in Aeschylus' *Eumenides*, played an important behind-the-scenes role in *Oedipus*, and appeared at the end of *Ion* to reveal decisive information about the hero's birth. Correspondingly, her role in the lived reality of Euripides' audience was still considerable. Obviously the authority and agency of these female characters would be filtered through the shared experience of ancient audiences, who were well aware of several visible and esteemed priestesses during this period.

If Euripides exploits his audience's familiarity with powerful sacerdotal women in their own social experience, how would they categorize Theonoe, who is suggestive of, but does not quite fit, the paradigm? Although she seems firmly rooted in Greek religion, she is not devoted to any specific god and thus resists categorization, setting her apart from other tragic priestesses who resemble historical figures more closely. In his survey of Euripidean priests, Richard Hamilton (1985: 64) remarks that Theonoe's rituals identify her as a priestess, rather than simply a prophet. Yet like the Pythia in *Ion*, who provides the tokens that enable Creusa to recognize her son, or Iphigenia, who uses her ritual authority to convince Thoas to let her go to the seashore with the precious cult statue of Artemis, Theonoe functions as a powerful plot agent. She is best understood in the framework of convention and disruption: a priestess, but of no particular god, and one who actually communicates with and influences Greek gods.

She is not only unique in the conventions of Euripidean priestess figures, but also unique within this play, for as Burnett (1971: 97) notices, she alone is truly tragic in that she is the only character who has to make an ethical choice, father over brother, a decision with consequences when her brother learns of her deception. In terms of the dualities of the play, the antithesis between the real and the seeming, Theonoe's unmediated access to the divine sphere aligns her, more than any character in the play, with *aether*, what she describes as "the pure breath of heaven's recess" (866) and what Sofer might consider to be "dark matter." Segal (1971: 243) identifies in her an "affinity with the highest and purest reality," in contrast to "the narrow, possessive localism" of Menelaus and Theoclymenus: "Her philosophical nature, as well as her femininity, separate her from the active, competitive, exclusively male functions of the polis with which Theoclymenus and Menelaus are associated." Euripides brings philosophical theory into play with Theonoe's access to *aether*, the intangible but pervasive divine consciousness. Suggesting a provocative consanguinity with the *eidolon*, the phantom Helen is fashioned from that same evanescent substance.

Just as she evokes a common paradigm, but also distorts it, Theonoe participates in a familiar set piece in tragedy, the *agon* (a debate or verbal contest), but in a distinctly unusual version of this common scene. Formal rhetorical debates in tragedy are reflective of the public discourse of Classical Athens, including the democratic assembly, and the law courts, where litigants, defendants, or prosecutors had equal time to present a speech in support of their case. Elton Barker in a book-length study (2009) of the device contextualizes the structured debates of tragedy within a continuum beginning with Homer. Examples can be found in Aeschylus' *Eumenides*: a debate between Apollo, who speaks in defense of Orestes, and the chorus of Furies (or their chorus leader), who acts as the prosecutor against the matricide; Athena arbitrates. We saw examples in *Oedipus*, including his intense confrontation with Creon in the second episode. There is wide variety in the format: for example, Sophocles creates a more conversational exchange in the confrontation between Creon and Antigone after she admits to performing burial rites for her brother. Most debates in tragedy are not in a legal setting and not all include a third actor as referee, but the *agon* does adhere to a balanced rhetorical structure, making the device seem artificial to modern audiences. Scholars are far from unanimous on defining or characterizing the tragic *agon*, although all three tragedians use some version of it. It is obvious that Euripides is especially fond of the structured debate; nearly all his surviving tragedies feature a formal *agon*. His *Trojan Women* furnishes a classic example. Set in the period immediately after the war, it represents a debate between the Trojan queen, Hecuba, who tries to persuade Menelaus to kill Helen, and Helen, who argues that she should return home with her husband. Both women deliver a structured *rhesis* (speech) of roughly the same length. Helen is the second to speak, which by convention suggests that she will prevail, and as we know, she does. A similar structure in the Theonoe scene becomes problematic when we realize that Helen and Menelaus are not dissenting with one another. Nonetheless they are given speeches of equal length, after which the chorus makes a comment, in keeping with the structure of the *agon* in *Trojan Women* and other Euripidean plays.

In his analysis of the scene, Kjeld Matthiessen (1968: 689–90) observes that even though Helen and Menelaus are arguing for the same goal, they contrast in their methods (see also Whitman 1974: 52–9). She supplicates Theonoe and appeals to her sense of justice; he threatens to kill Helen and himself. But the real contest is one that the audience cannot see, another variation of the antithesis between illusion and reality, and one that now implicates the limitations of the spectator's perception. From Theonoe's revelation we become aware of a divine *agon* in process: Hera represents the interests of Menelaus and Helen, Aphrodite of Theoclymenus, and Zeus as referee aligns with Theonoe. Matthiessen emphasizes the juridical aspects of Theonoe's decision. She declares herself to be most concerned with justice and claims direct access to a council of the gods where a court is in session (1968: 90). He compares the tribunal of the gods with the courtroom scene in Aeschylus' *Eumenides*, which features an arbitration by Athena of the competing claims of Apollo, in defense of Orestes, and the Erinyes (see also Marshall 2014: 38–9).

As this invisible court stages a corresponding *agon*, Helen and Menelaus each present arguments to the adjudicator. Helen's turns out to be most forceful since she is arguing in terms of transactions and obligations, and this concern with justice is the decisive argument as far as Theonoe is concerned. Helen was given to Proteus for safekeeping; even though he is deceased, his obligation still remains to return her (902–3). Theonoe chooses to privilege the wishes of her father over those of her brother and promises to remain silent, thereby supporting Hera's cause.

With *Oedipus* we saw how realistically Sophocles staged a triangulated conversation between his three actors. Euripides handles his third actor differently but no less effectively to emphasize a bond between husband and wife. Theonoe, played by the tritagonist, is a potential impediment, but her influence has an enormous implication for the other two speaking characters. In a second triangulated scene, her brother

Theoclymenus is similarly outside the orbit of the married couple, whose combined efforts are devoted to outsmarting him.

The Intrigue

The pattern of recognition and then deception, established by Aeschylus and varied by Euripides, is formulaic. In *Iphigenia in Tauris* the recognition scene is followed by an intrigue: the heroine devises a fictive ritual to deceive Thoas. The Theonoe episode disrupted audience expectations, but once her support has been obtained, the plot reverts to the pattern. Husband and wife must now concoct an escape plan. Menelaus again demonstrates the sad inadequacies of his Iliadic bluster: he wants to kill Theoclymenus, steal a chariot, and escape over land. Helen reveals a subtler mind when she suggests staging a mock funeral at sea. As Foley notes (2001: 319) by engaging in trickery (like Odysseus) Helen offers "an Odyssean critique" of the violence that is more typical of the *Iliad*.

Second Episode

The first episode ends here, marked formally by the long-delayed first stasimon performed while Helen begins her preparations to deceive Theoclymenus. The second episode (1165–1300) opens with the entry of the Egyptian king, who turns out to be more gullible than dangerous. In two short episodes, demarcated by three choral odes, Helen's plan is implemented. The action is framed by an ironic play-within-a-play that emphasizes costumes and identity, transformation and reversal, role-playing and stage-managing, all contributing to the tension between what is and what seems to be. Helen, now fully in control of the action, emerges from the *skene* in mourning garb ready to play her part. Theoclymenus enters from the *eisodos*, along with dogs—an unusual addition, but this is an unusual play—and attendants, who enter the building. He is easily duped into believing that Menelaus is the messenger of his own death; indeed the supposedly barbaric Egyptian king confounds expectations with his courteous and sensitive response to this fabricated news, even volunteering to give this "messenger" a decent set of clothes. Reversals abound. In the prologue Helen was a suppliant at the tomb of Proteus to protect herself from her suitor's advances and then at the knees of Theonoe to secure her cooperation; now she uses that same ritual to deceive Theoclymenus into supplying provisions for a fictive burial ritual at sea for Menelaus, in "empty weavings of robes" (1243). Enticed by the prospect of marrying the supposedly widowed Helen, he happily complies. Feigning ignorance in such matters, Helen lets her disguised husband enumerate all that is needed for the "funeral." The deceived is now the deceiver. Every item on his list from livestock to weapons, and of course a ship, will enable their escape and homeward journey. The play that began in a mournful tone for Helen's losses, both real and feared, now echoes that theme with a brilliant funerary parody.

Third Episode

The third episode, even shorter than the second, opens with a procession of attendants from the palace with the requested commodities. Among the most conspicuous would be the bed and bedsheets, the "empty weavings of robes" prescribed by Helen and requested by Menelaus (*strōta … lektra … kena*, "an empty bed, strewn with covers," 1261). Euripides' audience would have been familiar with Athenian obsequies for the unrecovered war dead, commemorated with such a procession and empty bed according to Thucydides (2.34.3, see also Burian 2007: 268). But they also know that this particular bed will serve a very different purpose for Helen and Menelaus, reunited after seventeen years. As Erika Weiberg (2020) notes, the play abounds with references to beds, especially empty beds, which function as a sign for the phantom Helen and evoke the famous signifier (the olive stump bed) of Odysseus and Penelope's marriage in their recognition scene. This is not the only ironic conflation of marriage and death in the scene. The motif is evoked again when Helen describes bathing, anointing, and dressing Menelaus within the palace (1382–5). These activities have ritual undertones: women prepared corpses for burial this way, but brides and grooms also took ritual baths in preparation for their weddings. On the other hand, the refreshing of Menelaus is also suggestive of the transformation of Odysseus (*Od.* 23.153–5), before he is recognized by Penelope. The end result, however we want to interpret the reference, is that Menelaus emerges from the *skene* building transformed and ready to take on his role as Helen's husband.

The episode prolongs the suspense and heightens the irony. Theoclymenus balks at letting Helen be present during the funeral at sea. She assures him: "I must honor my first marriage, and its nuptial intimacies" (1400). She hopes that the gods will grant him "the sorts of things I wish for you" and that he will have in her, "the sort of wife you should have in your house" (1407–8). She declines his offer of assistance on board, and he withdraws to the palace to prepare for his phantom bride, Paris-like in his delusion, as Helen in mourning garb, Menelaus in his new clothes, and their bed depart for the shore, "a paradox of wedding and funeral going on their way together" (Wolff 1973: 67).

That is the last the audience sees of the couple, but they are vividly recreated in the exodus speech by an Egyptian survivor of the fierce battle on board ship. Messenger speeches, like this one—replete with details such as the reluctant sacrificial bull, full of action including the bloody combat, and animated with direct speech by Helen and Menelaus—were plum roles, coveted by the most skillful actors, as we have already noted. It is quite likely that the protagonist, who had played the role of Helen, comes back as the messenger to reenact her escape for the audience. We will return to the final moments of the play to examine how Euripides resolves Theoclymenus' hostility to this news, but first a look at the chorus and then the physical elements of stagecraft will grant context and perspective.

The Chorus

The inventive handling of tragic conventions encompasses not just *Helen*'s plot and characters, but also its *choreia*, the heart and soul of tragedy. Like all other tragedians, Euripides wrote the music, and as *chorodidaskalos* he probably trained the choral performers for his plays. Euripides is associated with a style known as New Music, accessible to us only through a combination of metrical analysis and contemporary accounts.[12] According to the critiques put in the mouth of Aeschylus in Aristophanes' *Frogs*, Euripidean music was an excessively emotional, radical hodge-podge of different genres. From existing texts we discern devices such as alliteration and polyptoton (the repetition of words in different cases): Helen, for example, sings of *pathesi pathea, melesi melea*, "grief for grief, tune for tune" (174). Melisma, singing one syllable while moving between several different notes, was another characteristic of New Music. Scholarship has begun to reconstruct the sounds of classical tragedy, although there is much that is lost; the choreography of accompanying dances can only be imagined from the lyrics. Aristophanes' Aeschylus (*Frogs* 1328–9) complains that Euripidean choruses, infected by New Music, perform undignified or lascivious dances, although there is no evidence of this in *Helen*. Be that as it may, it is obvious that music defines the shape and rhythm of *Helen*. This, of course, is true for all tragedy, but *Helen*'s formal divisions are exceptionally delayed, compressed, and complicated by the pacing of these interludes. The postponed first stasimon creates an unexpectedly long first episode, while the cluster of three odes in the final four hundred lines punctuates the escape and prolongs the suspense. And it is not only choral songs that contribute to the structure of the drama. The action of the first episode is interrupted by a long duet between Helen and Menelaus, but even so there is a long interval (four hundred lines) of dramatic action without song and dance. Marshall (2014: 111) estimates that this would amount to roughly thirty to forty minutes of performance time without music.

The play requires a talented singing actor for the role of Helen, who initiates and participates in the parodos. (Early tragic roles may have consisted almost entirely of singing, Hall 2002: 4.) After the departure of Teucer at the end of the prologue, Helen begins her lament by summoning "winged girls, virgin daughters of Earth, Sirens" (167–78), mythical beings associated with death, in a dirge for her lost family and purportedly dead husband.[13] Greek women played conspicuous roles in lamentations, and so the parodos, by alluding to a familiar social performance, contributes to the funereal motif. When the chorus arrives, it is comprised of domestic slaves, captive Greek women, who were drying royal laundry on the riverbanks when they heard Helen's cries. It is a homely touch, and not without significance. If we entertain Marshall's (2014: 208) vision of the chorus shaking those "purple robes" (*phoinikas … peplous*) as they enter, the first intimation of the theme of cloth and clothing is given physical form. And this prop would also coordinate with the idea of Helen acting as a leader *in absentia* of Spartan maiden choirs, or *partheneia*, whose ritual dedication of garments is attested in songs composed by the seventh-century poet Alcman. In addition, the chorus of washerwomen might also evoke the "laundry songs," part of the tonal landscape of the ancient world; a single line of one is recorded by the second-century CE scholar Hephaestion: "I come back from the river with the shining garments" (PMG 385, discussed in Karanika 2014: 113).

Helen's prominent role in the parodos and her duet in the first episode are consistent with evidence for a diminution of the chorus in later tragedy. It also characterizes a shift in emphasis from choral lyrics to those of individual actors, typical of Euripides in this later period (although singing actors occur in late Sophocles too), and also a feature of New Music. Nothing is gratuitous here. Helen's duet with the chorus echoes and accentuates themes of the prologue: her disgrace and personal losses, and the futility and horror of the war.[14] And the analogy with Persephone is made explicit by Helen's wish that the goddess might send a mournful choir to accompany her dirge (175–8). A lyric exchange, or *kommos*, between actor and chorus is a relatively frequent phenomenon, for example the exchanges between Oedipus and the chorus discussed in the last chapter. And a *kommatic parodos*, such as this one, is not an uncommon way to bring in the chorus. It occurs in three of Sophocles' plays: *Electra*, *Philoctetes*, and *Oedipus at Colonus*. But this particular parodos is distinctive: Helen's lyrics are more numerous than those of the chorus; atypically, she sings the first strophe, or stanza; they join in response with lyrics whose meters are very closely aligned with hers.

Euripides shows a distinct preference for female choruses, who serve as confidantes and advisors to his principal female characters. On the most obvious level, the chorus contributes to the female focus of the drama. As companions of Helen, the women are consistent with the female solidarity of several other tragic choruses. With the exception of the young virgins who act as Deianeira's support group in Sophocles' *Women of Trachis*, this female homosocial bond between character and chorus is characteristically Euripidean. It includes the sympathetic women friends of Phaedra in Euripides' *Hippolytus*, the Athenian attendants of Creusa in his *Ion*, and even (up to a point) the chorus of Corinthian women in *Medea*. The chorus of *Andromeda* is likewise comprised of enslaved women, although not Greek, to the royal household. These female friendships, usually between aristocratic female characters and lower status choruses, often lead to secretive complicity: for example the chorus of *Hippolytus*, sworn to secrecy by Phaedra, remains silent when Theseus reads out her suicide letter falsely accusing Hippolytus of rape. In *Helen*, however, the female bond is salutary and reaffirms marriage and the patriarchal order. Although it never does more than advise and sympathize, which is within the range of normative choral behaviors, it overturns conventions by entering the *skene* with Helen early in the first episode. And in the exodus, the chorus leader steps forward to dissuade Theoclymenus from killing his sister. The act is so unusual that editors have suspected a scribal error (e.g., Burian 2007: 289), but for a play so full of surprises and witty inventions an emendation that gives the lines to an anonymous servant fails to understand how consonant this remarkable intervention is with the tone of the drama.

Turning now to the choral odes, we observe a highly embellished, decorative style, typical of late Euripidean drama and the innovations of New Music. This includes the phenomenon of "choral projection," whereby a tragic chorus alludes to or behaves like choruses of other genres, for example the *partheneia*, or cultic "maiden songs" performed by choirs of girls (Steiner 2011: 299). The stasima, clustered in the final third of the play, share several themes. Christian Wolff (1973) identifies the antithesis of *eros* and death and notes that Helen is at the center of all three odes (69–77). Choral reflections progress from the tragedy of war in the first stasimon to the prospect of marriage in the third. The theme of music, festival, and ritual also links the songs. And in various ways the songs contrast, reflect, or enhance the stage action.

First Stasimon

The long first episode ends on a note of optimism and hope, as Helen and Menelaus secure their escape. The mood is tempered by the delayed first stasimon (1107), a sober reflection on the tragedy of a futile war that could have been prevented by negotiations (*logois*, 1159). The chorus sings of the grief of the Greek wives who cut their hair in mourning for their husbands lost in the war (1121–6), a counterpoint to the feigned mourning of Helen, who at that very moment is within the palace cutting off her hair as she pretends to mourn her husband's death. The subsequent stasima are more sanguine with a focus on music and festivals.

Second Stasimon

The second stasimon, performed after Helen has duped Theoclymenus into believing that she will marry him, is a curiosity. There are textual problems that contribute to the opacity of the language and its relationship to the action, but there are other enigmas as well. An eclectic hymn to the Great Mother (known as Cybele), its narrative melds elements of the myth of Demeter and Persephone with cultic details of the worship of the foreign goddess who had recently been incorporated into the state religion of Athens; there are references to the cult of Dionysus as well. The song imagines a distraught mother goddess in a chariot drawn by beasts, the signature conveyance of Cybele, and then being reconciled in a festive context with her daughter, "who cannot be named" (1307). The song epitomizes the trend toward syncretism, the blending of different cultic or mythic qualities of two distinctly different deities, a feature of Greek religion that seems to have fascinated Euripides. But it is difficult to ascertain why he chose to highlight this amalgamation here. More serious objections are that the ode suffers an apparent disconnection from the events of the play; it has been adduced as an *embolimon*, a choral song that can be "thrown into" a drama without regard for its relevance (e.g., Whitman 1974: 65; Burian 2007: 270). This was apparently a characteristic of Agathon's choral odes, and those of later tragedy, although there is not much surviving evidence of this. While it is true that Aristotle preferred a chorus more tightly integrated with the drama, and decried irrelevant choral odes, this is not a charge that he levels against Euripides. Accusations of irrelevance overlook this ode's points of contact with dramatic events; for example, it describes Aphrodite's enjoyment of song, which implicitly mitigates her displeasure at Helen's fidelity to Menelaus. The text of the final stanza is corrupt, but there seems to be criticism of Helen for neglecting the worship of this nameless but powerful goddess, perhaps offering an explanation for her wrath and Helen's separation from her husband.

The song picks up elements of the references to Demeter and Persephone introduced in the parodos, completing the mythic narrative trajectory by metaphorically resurrecting a Persephone figure. This makes the ode's narrative pattern akin to the *anodos* motif of the drama. Recent critics have offered other productive solutions to the apparent puzzles of the ode. Laura Swift suggests that the entire tragedy refers to elements of a *partheneion* or "maiden song." The second stasimon is thus consonant with the play, which produces, by Swift's reckoning (2010: 434), an "extended metaphor for female sexuality and the transition to sexual maturity."

Third Stasimon

The third and final stasimon, performed as Helen and Menelaus, are on board their purloined vessel and preparing to escape, features novelties associated with New Music. Tightly bound to the action, it reflects the successful journey and homecoming of the couple in a conventional poetic format known as a *propemptikon*, a "bon voyage" song. A charming specimen of Euripidean escapist lyricism, the song invokes the Phoenician ship transporting the reunited couple homeward and summons the ship as "chorus leader" of the dancing dolphins that follow (deriving from the belief that they were dancing to the flute player who set the rowing beat on a Greek ship). These allusions are suggestive of the dithyramb, an early form of choral dance still included in the festivals of Dionysus, and associated with the birth of tragedy. In an imaginative and learned reconstruction of the ode's choreography, Deborah Steiner (2011) suggests that the chorus of *Helen* would arrange in a circle, the formation of the dithyramb, around the flute player as they sang these words. It is also possible, as Steiner suggests, that the flute player could whirl about as well, a behavior described disapprovingly by Aristotle (*Poet.* 1461b30). The second stanza (or first antistrophe) is self-reflexive, a choral performance describing other choral performances in Sparta, and imagines Helen returning home to local festivals, ritual processions (*komoi*), choruses (*choroi*), and the wedding of her daughter Hermione.

The second strophe (or third stanza) is a variation on the "escape" ode format, shared with several Euripidean tragedies (Padel 1974). It is especially poignant in this context, since while Helen is able to take flight with her husband, the chorus of Greek women remains in captivity. Indeed their assistance in the deception of Theoclymenus puts their lives at risk, although they are mercifully spared through the intervention of the Dioscuri. The impossible wish of flying like a flock of Libyan birds, visualized as a type of chorus following a piper and winging its way to the streams of the Spartan river Eurotas, is matched in the corresponding antistrophe by the fantasy of the winged horses of the Dioscuri, "under the whirling of the shining stars," protectors of sea voyagers, descending to watch over their sister's ship and then rehabilitating her reputation when she returns home. The final stanza thus returns to the marine theme of the first part of the ode and looks forward to, or even produces, the epiphany of the twins in the final moments of the play.

Organically linked to the action of the drama, the ode articulates the happy fulfillment of Helen's escape and homecoming with appealing details from the natural world, dancing dolphins, a chorus of long-necked birds, and whirling constellations, as well as promises of festivals, family, and restored dignity for Helen. It is the final lyric and choreographic performance of the play, an upbeat finale that sets the mood for the messenger's report in the exodus of Helen and Menelaus' audacious departure.

While the choral odes are reduced in number—compare, for example, the five odes (including the parodos) of *Oedipus*—and replaced by intricate lyric arias by Helen, the chorus is

still an important musical element. Their duet with Helen
illuminates their close bond with the heroine, and taken as a
whole the choral lyrics present a unified progression of emotion
that enhances the affective arc of the drama, moving from
the dirges of the parodos, the lament for the war in the first
stasimon, the encapsulation of the *anodos* motif in the second,
and finally the cheerful anticipation of the third stasimon.
Moreover their songs have the potential for innovative musical
and choreographic elements that might include the *auletes*,
whose role is charmingly mirrored by the piper leading the
flock of Libyan cranes.

The Spectacle

A group of fifteen chorus members would be a substantial
component of the spectacle of the drama, even when they
are silent. We resort to conjectures about their costumes, but
surviving visual culture provides some guidance. A marble relief
from Piraeus (now in the Athens National Museum), dating
from the late fifth century, shows what appear to be *choreutae*
holding their masks (Wyles 2011: 17–18). The young men
wear long-sleeved robes, cinched at the waist, which would
be appropriate for the Greek chorus women of *Helen*. Like all
costumes in tragedy, theirs would not be realistic versions of
contemporary clothing, but they could certainly denote age,
status, gender, and ethnicity. For example, it would be entirely
appropriate to think of them wearing saffron robes. These
young maidens evoke the virginal choruses of ancient Greece,
whose cultic garments were a brilliant yellow or orange, a
color traditionally associated with coming of age.

With the exception of his *Bacchae*, no other Euripidean
play puts such strong emphasis on costume, an important
component of *opsis* ("spectacle"), and an opportunity for the
choregos, or citizen sponsor, to gain prestige. Although this
ephemeral production element is lost, the text supplies some

clues. We know that Helen wears white garments (probably linen) as a suppliant and changes into black for her feigned mourning, a rare costume change in Greek tragedy. Her robe would cover her arms, which distinguishes her costume from clothing worn by real Greek women of the time, and perhaps signifies that she is a figure from the past.[15] Other details can be extrapolated from visual art contemporary with the play, although these suggest a number of possibilities for Theonoe. Three complementary factors need to be considered: ethnicity, religious status, and the date of the play. Wyles examines evidence for more exotic accouterments to signify ethnicity in the costumes of tragic characters. For example, an Attic calyx krater dating from around 400 BCE, inspired by Euripides' *Andromeda*, depicts the Ethiopian princess wearing a hooded headdress that identifies her as non-Greek, although her long-sleeved, ornately decorated garment is typical of tragedies produced in this period. Would an Athenian audience have recognized other sartorial features as specifically priestly? Scholarship on this question suggests not, since Athenian priestesses, unlike their male counterparts, seem to have worn ordinary clothing (Brøns 2016: 274–300). It is relevant that an early fourth-century vase depicting a scene from of *Iphigenia in Tauris* shows the priestess in a garment embellished with woven patterns, characteristic of tragic costumes in this period. Putting this all together we can speculate that in her short period before the audience, Theonoe wore some kind of headdress to signify her ethnicity, and an ornate robe suited to her status as the daughter of a wealthy household.

In a drama predicated on a phantom version of its heroine, a drama that articulates an invisible, ethereal dimension of consciousness, the very notion of materiality becomes highly charged. In this mutable universe of sensory perception, clothing and textiles possess a transformative power to conceal and restore status or deceptively imbue bodies with social meaning. Menelaus looks like a beggar but reestablishes his heroic identity through costume; Helen changes into widow's weeds to preserve her marriage. It is an instability that extends

as well to stage properties and buildings. A funeral bed silently
but insistently declares its true purpose as it is carried away.
A physical ambiguity correspondingly encompasses the very
architecture of the theater and its permanent—and notionally
stable—features. Consider the tomb of Proteus, where Helen
takes up occupancy in the prologue. In no other extant tragedy
does supplication occur at a tomb; it is more appropriately
conducted at an altar as in Sophocles' *Oedipus*. Positioned in
the orchestra in the original production, the tomb was probably
represented by, or occupied the space of, the *thymele*, the altar
of Dionysus in the center of the orchestra, now transformed
through language into a cenotaph, and even standing for
the deceased Proteus, who continues to protect the woman
given into his care seventeen years earlier. Helen's ritual is
consequently an implicit acknowledgment of the structure's
extra-dramatic status. It remains a focus throughout the first
half of the play, shielding Helen in her suppliant contact.
Her position in the orchestra ensures that she will be in the
midst of the chorus with whom she sings the parodos when
the group enters, their physical proximity emphasizing their
friendship. The tomb continues to emanate its beneficent force,
even signifying the fidelity of Helen who convinces Menelaus
of her chastity by pointing to her pathetic bed of straw beside
it (797–9) (Weiberg 2020: 11–12).

The other significant structure of course is the *skene*. In
Oedipus Tyrannus, as we have seen, the wooden building
represents the royal palace of Thebes, but its interior spaces
also signify Oedipus' emotional and psychic condition. In a
different manner, but equally as complex, the *skene* of *Helen*
is saturated with a complex meaning. Helen indicates that it
represents the palace of the royal family, and yet any association
with domesticity or a private realm, as in *Oedipus* and other
plays, is muted or even absent. In Teucer's words (68–70) the
palace is "fortified," "fitted with regal enclosures and stone
foundations," like the house of Ploutos (the wealthy god of the
dead). Menelaus, when he arrives, re-emphasizes the grandeur
and wealth of the palace (430–1), perhaps inviting the audience

to imagine these features on the exterior of an unadorned *skene*. There are good reasons to believe, despite the Aristotelian reference to *skenographia*, that Euripides expected his Athenian audience to visualize these features (Allan 2008: 157–8).

A blank slate, a lack of adornment on the exterior of the wooden *skene* building, had several advantages, the most pertinent being that the structure absorbs the mood of the moment. The *skene* becomes especially interesting and meaningful when the chorus advises Helen to consult the "oracles of the virgin" in the palace and accompanies her within. It is thus to a house full of women that Menelaus presents himself; even the doorkeeper, who denies him access, is a woman. And while the inner spaces are now decidedly feminine, these are not conventional domestic spaces. This interior is not only gendered as female at this point—and will remain exclusively so until line 1300 when Theoclymenus sends his hunting dogs and attendants inside—but is also designated as an oracular temple that houses a priestess who is able to tell Helen and her attendants that Menelaus not only lives, but will arrive in Egypt after his trials at sea. The fact that Menelaus cannot enter intensifies the impression that this space is sacred and only admissible to a select group.

A comparison of the building that Theonoe occupies with those of priestesses in the two similar Euripidean plays is illuminating. In *Iphigenia in Tauris*, the *skene* represents the temple of Artemis. Likewise *Ion* is set before the temple of Apollo at Delphi. The virginal Delphic priestess, like Theonoe, provides oracles from within the *skene*. Having the structure represent the inner sanctum of a priestess in *Helen* is consonant with these plays, but contrastingly the semiotics of this interior space fluctuates. For the first half of the play it is Theonoe's domain. Unlike Iphigenia, priestess of Artemis, or the Pythia, priestess of Apollo, Theonoe is not in a temple, nor does she have a specific sacerdotal role. Or to put it another way, she is not the priestess of any specific deity, unlike Iphigenia and the Pythia, and therefore would not be connected with a temple. But within her uniquely sacred space she has a direct connection with the gods, communicating with and influencing them. In this invisible interior Theonoe accesses the refined *aether* of pure knowledge and participates in a divine assembly that has a direct effect on the action of the play.

It is appropriate in a play about illusion and insubstantiality that the nature of the stage building is not entirely stable. Once Theonoe has played her part, the sacredness of the building dissolves, as it were; it then becomes the site of deception and role-playing, reverting to its original function. When Helen next enters the royal house, it becomes a dressing room, paralleling the function of the space in the production of the drama, and she emerges in mourning garb, ready to play her part; Menelaus follows suit. Like the tomb/altar, the *skene* allows its extra-dramatic function to show through. Later tragedies do not feature scene changes; although Aeschylus allowed the *skene* to serve first as the temple of Apollo at Delphi, and then shifted the stage action to Athens, other extant dramas maintain a stable location. With *Helen*, however, Euripides manipulates the symbolism of the *skene* to create a series of shifting spatial meanings. Its final status is as a protective enclosure for Theonoe when the *coryphaeus* apparently restrains Theoclymenus from entering, a reproduction of the earlier interaction between the female doorkeeper and Menelaus (Stavrinou 2015: 122–3).

The *skene* building, or rather its flat roof, becomes a focus in the exodus of the play as it does in several other tragedies. Euripides had a fondness for the *deus ex machina*, literally "the god from the machine," to end his dramas, although it is not simply the convenient form of closure that Aristotle disparages (*Poet.* 1454a37-b6, cf. Horace *Ars Poetica* 191–2). When Theoclymenus vows to kill Theonoe and the chorus leader who tries to defend her (1495–1511), Helen's twin brothers, the Dioscuri, descend onto the roof of the *skene* (as they also do in Euripides' *Electra*), to the area described by Pollux (4.127) as the *theologeion*, "the divine speaking place." This stunt was probably accomplished by a crane to which actors were strapped or possibly in this case a platform holding the two actors (one of whom would be a non-speaking character), lowered onto the flat *skene* roof.[16] It is widely accepted that the *mechane* was in existence by 431 BCE: the first known occurrence is Medea appearing in a dragon-drawn chariot with the bodies of her dead sons. There are several scenes in tragedy, other than the exodus, when actors in the roles of gods or semi-divine beings speak from the *theologeion*. Euripides certainly did not have a monopoly on the practice, but he does seem to have utilized the space and the crane for spectacular effects not found in his rivals. Halfway through his *Heracles*, for example, two malevolent spirits descend to inflict madness on the eponymous hero. *Andromeda*, produced in the same package as *Helen*, used the crane for an equally an impressive effect: Perseus and some replica of his horse Bellerophon (fr. 124 and 306–8) descend to rescue the captive princess. Aristophanes' parody the following year in his *Thesmophoriazusae* suggests that it was a memorable *coup de théâtre*.

The descent of Perseus occurs before the conclusion of *Andromeda*, but Euripides uses the crane most often in the exodus, as a *deus ex machina*. Close examination challenges the reproach that the device is a desperate means of resolving a plot. Medea's eerie appearance above Jason emphasizes her supernatural abilities, which he foolishly ignored, and marks her separation from the human realm as she cruelly denies him any contact with the corpses of his sons. When Artemis appears to the dying Hippolytus and his father Theseus, the tragic action is complete. She has come to help him understand the reason for his suffering, with details that the audience already knows from the prologue, i.e., that Aphrodite is responsible for the youth's tragic demise. In *IT* Athena does intervene to prevent Thoas from pursuing Iphigenia by ship, but only because Euripides creates a situation in which he can, a complication that is entirely unnecessary for the resolution of the plot. In *Helen*, the ship carrying the reunited couple and their supporters is well on its way back to Greece, and the plot is essentially resolved when the Dioscuri appear; their intercession is, as Francis Dunn (1995: 142) puts it, an "irrelevant epiphany." On the other hand the effect would be to expand the dramatic space and remind the audience of the divine backdrop to the story.

Women, Ritual, and Audiences

One notable feature of these epiphanies by crane is they frequently prescribe some religious practice, often to commemorate the principal character. The institution of cults, rituals, priesthoods, or shrines recommended in these final moments presumably connect the fictive world of the drama with the lived reality of its audience. *Iphigenia in Tauris* ends with the intercession of Athena, who ordains cults and sanctuaries for Orestes and Iphigenia in Greece. Similarly Castor delivers his cease and desist order, which Theoclymenus obligingly promises to obey, and then turns his attention to Helen. He promises that after her death she "will be called a goddess" (1666–7); her divinity, which was part of her tradition, especially in Sparta, is now a reward for her virtue. Castor also includes Helen (1668) in a *theoxenia*, a special "god feast," which honored the twins, a form of worship attested for this period (Allan 2008: 342).

Throughout his oeuvre Euripides displays a keen interest in the history of Greek religion, supplying numerous details of obscure observances. There is debate about whether the poet fabricates or distorts details of rituals and cults (e.g., Dunn 1995: 60–5), although it must be acknowledged that much remains unknown about the more arcane practices of Greek religion. Donald Mastronarde (2010: 183n. 58) prudently suggests that any aetiology (or origin story) in Euripides has "some point of contact" with what his audience knows. In *Helen*, Castor's inclusion of his sister in the ritual hospitality may well be Euripides' invention, but his Athenian audience would have been familiar with the *theoxenia* for Castor and Pollux. It would not be much of a stretch to include Helen in the celebration.

At any rate, the reference to Helen's divinity is the final detail in a play that has highlighted the religious roles and ritual lives of women, both implicitly and explicitly. The prospect of a divinized Helen resonates with historical evidence for her worship, especially in Sparta where maiden choruses danced in her honor (Dillon 2002: 211–14), a cultic identity intimated by her close interaction with the chorus of this tragedy. Sheila Murnaghan (2016: 164) identifies Helen in Egypt, as a "dislocated choral leader" whose return home will restore normative choral performances. Other aspects of women's ritual identities complement these allusions. The reunion of the mother goddess with her daughter celebrated in the second stasimon had a special relevance. An important event in the ritual lives of Greek women was the Thesmophoria, an annual festival in honor of the reunion of Demeter and her daughter, the setting for Aristophanes' comedic parody of *Helen* the following year.

These details are consonant with Euripidean tragedy in the last decade or so of his life, when he indicates a scholarly interest in women's religious activities. It is true that tragedy of all periods is infused with religious concerns, for example the prayers of Eteocles and the chorus in the *Seven*, and the supplications in *Oedipus*. Euripides, however, is exceptionally detailed and realistic in his representations of cults, ceremonies, and forms of worship; the historicity of his depiction of religion has been well documented (for example Mikalson 1991). These embedded rituals, prayers, hymns, and the like reflect the importance of religion in the public and private lives of Euripides' audiences. Most religious activities were connected in some way with the polis, which, according to a widely accepted view, "anchored, legitimated, and mediated all religious activity," including cults and festivals (Sourvinou-Inwood 1990: 297). Euripides' dramas, produced at civic festivals of Dionysus, are embedded in and reflect this system. Tragedy, born of ritual and enacted in a ritual context, consistently explores the power of ritual to shape and give meaning to human experiences. By including familiar religious acts and agents within its fictive world, tragedy considers the performative quality of ritual in a way that aligns those acts with the fictional world of drama. For instance, Helen's ruse depended on a reenactment of a funerary ritual, one that Menelaus seemed to invent ad hoc as he listed the commodities required for a voyage homeward and yet which also mirrored a civic ritual familiar to an Athenian audience. She changed her appearance to signify her participation in the rites of mourning, masqueraded as a grieving widow, and stage-managed her way to freedom by adapting religious acts for her own ends.

Euripides often provides his memorable female characters with this kind of powerful ritual agency: e.g., the disruptive celebrants of Dionysus in *Bacchae*, the authoritative priestess-heroine of *Iphigenia in Tauris*, or the powerful seer Theonoe in *Helen*. Although his mythical fictions reproduce social restrictions of Greek women, they also reflect their high status in religion. A fragment (494 K) of his *Captive Melanippe* claims that women have the "greatest part in divine affairs." The speaker lists holy offices at oracles and other sacred duties. The visual record (especially pottery) supports these claims with depictions of women engaging in the full spectrum of religious activities including processions, prayers, and sacrifices: Joan Breton Connelly's superb catalogue (2007), for example, surveys the representation of priestesses in the plastic arts. Such available evidence indicates that the authority of Euripidean heroines in later plays coheres with historical women's ritual identities, which were increasingly visible in the late fifth century and conferred status, independence, and influence.

There is a distinct specificity about how Euripides embeds or refers to women's ritual, especially in the plays of his later years. The female chorus of his *Electra* (produced between 420 and 415) offers the morose heroine clothing for a festival of Hera in Argos (190–4), a historically documented event. And there are several references to Athenian women's cultic weaving of Athena's robe for the Panathenaic festival and procession in these later plays. Trojan women imagine preparing Athena's robe for the occasion in Euripides' *Hecuba* (463–74), a contrast with their apocalyptic world. Iphigenia laments not being able to participate in the same ritual activity (*IT* 218–24). Scholars are divided on whether or not the maenadic cult depicted in *Bacchae* is as shocking as Euripides' depiction, but there is little doubt that women engaged in the cult in some way (see Versnel 1990).

This leads to speculations about the target audience of plays such as *Helen*, *Iphigenia in Tauris*, and *Ion*. Historians of Greek tragedy have few doubts that women were in the audience, challenging earlier theories that they could not attend (reviewed by Rosseli 2011: 158–94), but there has been little attention to their reception of the dramatic representation of women. When Aristophanes dramatizes their hostility toward Euripides in his *Thesmophoriazusae*, he has devised a creative way to parody Euripides that assumes a female audience. Aristophanes has the women of Athens conspire to assassinate Euripides at their annual festival because the tragic poet has revealed their infidelities and misdemeanors in his plays—the implication of course is that they have seen his plays and have responded as literary critics of a particularly dangerous bent. Certainly characters such as the child-killing Medea, the frenzied Agave who rips apart her son in *Bacchae*, or Phaedra with a fatal desire for her stepson Hippolytus, contribute to Euripides' reputation for misogyny, but more careful analysis reveals his sensitive understanding of women's lives. And of course the characters of Helen (in this play) and Iphigenia (in *IT*) are heroic, virtuous, and intelligent. Aristophanes rescues his "Euripides" from the murderous women by having him promise to write better versions of them—precisely what he has done in *Helen*, which Aristophanes parodies in his comedy (Fletcher 2012: 219). He very cleverly makes it seem that Euripides' female audience demanded this new form of drama, and they do so in the same ritual context (i.e., the worship of Demeter reunited with her daughter) that informs *Helen*. Laurie O'Higgins (2007: 159–60) has argued that Aristophanes was engaging with his female audience in this play, a speculation that could also accommodate the possibility of a strong female presence in Euripides' production the year before. In a city-state that had recently lost thousands of its male citizens to war, it is conceivable that women occupied a significant number of seats in the theater of Dionysus in 412 BCE.

Relatedly, tragedy, even though it acknowledges the ideal of socially muted women, also represents women traveling in the context of ritual. The chorus of Athenian serving women in *Ion* participates in *theoria* (religious tourism) at Delphi. That of *Phoenician Women* is on its way to serve at Delphi. The chorus of *Bacchae* brings the rites of Dionysus from the East, while the women of Thebes relocate to the neighboring mountains to perform them (Konstantinou 2018). Kowalzig (2016) argues that the chorus of *IT*, Greek maidens trapped in barbaric Tauris, mediates between different ancient Mediterranean religious traditions to produce "transcultural chorality." Weiss (2018: 181) draws attention to the "metamusical" aspect of *choreia* (song and dance) in *Helen* in the context of travel. And when Euripides situates women's religious identities beyond Athens in a Panhellenic setting, he not only suggests a more expansive picture of women's lives but also moves beyond exclusively Athenocentric concerns to appeal to a wider audience.

Beyond Athens

The preceding chapters have considered tragedy in the civic context of fifth-century Athenian democracy, but our survey would not be complete without acknowledging venues both within Attica and in the Mediterranean World beyond. The brevity of the foregoing discussion does not do full justice to the recent proliferation of scholarship on the topic of the theater in other parts of the ancient world. It is beyond dispute that tragedy was popular throughout the Mediterranean, probably from its earliest history; the numerous stone theaters at sites in Sicily, the Black Sea area, and North Africa are testimony to the genre's wide-ranging audiences in antiquity. The most recent and authoritative collection and analysis of this evidence, by two of the most esteemed historians of ancient drama, Eric Csapo and Peter Wilson (2020), moves away from an Athenocentric model of theater culture to envision a robust and widespread theater culture both in Attica, the area surrounding Athens, and further afield. By the end of the fifth century tragedies were reproduced in over twenty dramatic festivals in deme theaters, i.e., the hinterlands of Athens. Several of these had a seating capacity in excess of the local populations (even including women and slaves), which might suggest audiences coming from other parts of Attica (Csapo and Wilson 2020: 12–13). It would be a mistake to discount these venues as "second-rate," since there is evidence that all of the three most celebrated tragedians participated in some of their productions. One of these venues, the oldest stone theater of the ancient world in Thorikos (facing the Aegean Sea to the south), dates from the beginning of the fifth century; the celebrated actor Theodorus performed there in a fourth-century production. Tragedy had a more international appeal as well. Vases from Sicily including ones depicting scenes from Euripides' *Medea* and *Iphigenia in Tauris* attest to the popularity of tragedy on the island. Although the story is likely apocryphal, Plutarch's account (*Nicias* 29) of Athenian survivors of the naval disaster of 415 BCE, who were granted their freedom by reciting Euripides before the Sicilians, is not implausible. There is also considerable evidence that in the last quarter of the fifth century plays were reproduced in the Black Sea area (Braund, Hall, and Wyles 2020) and at numerous locales throughout the Mediterranean. Edmund Stewart speculates that tragedy contributed to "an interconnected network of festivals, linked through travel" (2017: 94). His suggestion that Euripides wrote "travel plays" specifically for foreign audiences is conjectural, but he does identify a significant theme in plays such as *Helen* set outside the Greek world. To understand tragedy as an ancient genre therefore we must acknowledge that its wide dissemination throughout the ancient Mediterranean attests to its ability to represent issues of individual choice, family conflict, and unseen forces—dark matter, fate, or the gods, whatever term one prefers—that entertained a wide variety of audiences and gave meaning to their lives.

Epilogue: Post-classical Tragedy

Tragedy did not die with Sophocles' *Oedipus at Colonus* but continued to be written and produced in Athens during the fourth century, although nothing remains of these later dramas. Aristotle's *Poetics* (*c*. 335 BCE) makes it obvious that copies of fifth-century tragedies circulated in his day. By 340 BCE revivals of classical tragedies—Euripides was especially popular—become part of the dramatic contests, which may have lost their religious affiliations by this time (Garland 2004: 13). The acting profession had become more established: by the mid-fifth century a prize for acting was instituted, and by the end of the century acting guilds regulated and protected their members. It was during this century that actors, keen to magnify their roles, emended the scripts in circulation; their interpolations crept into the texts of Aeschylus, Sophocles, and Euripides and continue to exercise classical philologists. The Athenian statesman Lycurgus, also responsible for the permanent stone theater of Dionysus, passed a decree that stabilized the texts and created a repository for their official copies.

Aristotle's advice (*Poet*. 1455a) to contemporary dramatists indicates that the genre was still very much alive in the late fourth century; nearly half of the examples that he cites in his *Poetics* are post-classical. Sadly not a single complete specimen survives, with the probable exception of *Rhesus*, "an embarrassment, both for its defenders and for its detractors" (Liapis 2012: v); its Euripidean authorship was contested even in antiquity. On the other hand, it would be a mistake to close any discussion of tragedy without acknowledging its well-attested survival in the fourth century, as a plethora of titles and fragments indicate: among the most frequently cited are Astydamas, Chaeremon, and Theodectus. Georgia Xanthakis-Karamanos (1980) has assembled the evidence for later tragedy, and subsequent scholars have refined her contributions. Wright (2016: 118–20), for example, disputes her conclusion that later tragedy was a decadent, or more emotional, variation of the classical ideal. And to judge from the surviving fragments and titles, these later tragic poets treated many of the same mythical themes as their predecessors. It also seems that the number of non-Athenian tragedians increased during this period (Garland 2004: 13), although fragments from the fifth-century poet Ion of Chios demonstrate that this was not an exclusively fourth-century phenomenon.

Much of twentieth- and twenty-first-century scholarship has supported the notion that tragedy went into a period of decay in the fourth century—a premise that was difficult to dispute in the absence of any textual evidence of its survival, but equally as difficult to prove. The theory was that with the loss of its empire and hegemonic position, Athenian culture went into decline and that surviving theaters were devoted to reproductions of canonical fifth-century works. This hypothesis has been rigorously tested in a collection of essays whose introduction contends that unquestioning acceptance of the death of tragedy in so much of recent scholarship is based on a prevailing paradigm that posits a single performance in Athens during the fifth century. It is a model that became dogma not only because fourth-century pundits, including Aristotle, canonized fifth-century tragedy, but also because recent scholars ignore the abundant evidence for a flourishing theatrical culture in the fourth century. A new paradigm that considers a "multi-cultural, interconnected and networked

Mediterranean" (Csapo, Goette, Green, and Wilson 2014: 5) has developed from recent trends in cultural studies that break down barriers between different disciplines. As fresh evidence for the production of tragedy comes to light, and new methodologies are applied to existing evidence, the study of this timeless genre continues to evolve.

NOTES

Chapter 1

1   There are speculations that *Prometheus Bound* was not by Aeschylus and that *Rhesus* was not by Euripides. Euripides' *Alcestis* is considered to be a pro-satyric drama (i.e., produced in lieu of a satyr drama) but has the form of a tragedy and is included in the total number of tragic texts.

2   Sourvinou-Inwood (2003: 67–200) argues that the festival began as a ritual for the advent of Dionysus which began with a sacrifice of a goat.

3   Wright (2016) provides an accessible collection of the fragments of the lost tragedians with translations and a useful analysis.

4   A fragment (fr.8) of Phrynichus has a eunuch getting chairs ready for a council meeting and describing them as being ready for the Persians who have "long since gone to Greece," which Aeschylus quotes in his opening line (Sommerstein 2010: 45).

5   The term is often misunderstood: it means getting pleasure from causing others harm, and had a legal connotation for the ancient Athenians.

6   Testimonia are supplied by Csapo and Slater (2010: 120–1), who also offer other possible arrangements of events (107).

Chapter 2

1   An example of the dochmiac: The wise kangaroos/prefer boots to shoes. ∪ – – ∪ – ⋮ ∪ – – ∪ –. There is a preponderance of long syllables and any shorts (∪) can be replaced by a long syllable.

2   Zeitlin's (1978) essay on the dynamics of misogyny
     in Aeschylus' trilogy remains a forceful and relevant
     interpretation.

3   Agamemnon's father, Atreus, tricked his brother into eating
     his own children in revenge for Thyestes' seduction of Atreus'
     wife.

4   Some scholars are inclined to delete the line as spurious, while
     others suspect that subsequent lines referring to the remaining
     pieces of armor have somehow been deleted. Taplin (1977:
     159–62) wants to delete the reference to greaves and speculates
     that Eteocles would already be armed. Hutchinson (1985:
     153), who considers an arming scene to be "cumbrous and
     distracting," reviews the philology of the scene.

Chapter 3

1   Wright (2016: 97–100) helps to fill in the gaps with a
     speculative analysis of Philocles' work, based on titles and
     mentions in comedy, and his possible rivalry with Sophocles.

2   On ancient variants, and the melding of curse and oracle, see
     further: L. Edmonds (1985: 6–9).

3   For a sensible treatment of the significance of the absence of
     the curse targeting Pelops in *Oedipus*, and the bibliography on
     the topic, see Sewell-Rutter (2007: 126–8).

4   Goward (1999: 26–32) discusses the features of Sophoclean
     message narratives, although she does not include this speech
     among her list (170n.7). Of the items in her list, Oedipus'
     speech only lacks direct discourse.

5   The precise translation of the Greek is: "with one blow by the
     staff by means of (*ek*) this hand." In other words the deictic
     tēsde modifies the genitive *kherios*, "hand."

6   Euripides' *Hecuba* ends with the blinding of Polymestor, his
     Cyclops with the blinding of Polyphemus. The following
     chapter will discuss a third example of a mask change in his
     Helen.

7 See for example the comments of Taplin (1977: 89) on the mask (and 110) on the possible use of the *ekkyklema* for the tableau. Dawe (2006: 184) is more convinced and convincing about the likelihood of the *ekkyklema*.

8 These figures are calculated by Esposito (1996: 85), who omits *Prometheus Bound* (probably not by Aeschylus), which has a smaller amount of choral lyric.

9 We find similar civic collective choruses in Aeschylus' *Agamemnon* and *Persians*; Sophocles' *OC* and *Antigone*; Euripides' *Heracles*, *Heracleidae*, and *Alcestis*.

10 Scodel (1982) provides a compact but insightful analysis of the thematic organization.

11 The original manuscript reads *hubris phuteuei tyrannon* "Hubris begets tyranny." Dawe accepts an emendation that changes the syntax: *hubrin phuteuei tyrannis* "Tyranny begets hubris," but Wilson and Lloyd-Jones accept the manuscript reading in their authoritative Oxford Classical Text.

12 Carey (1986: 176) gives a comprehensive survey of the use of the term in Greek literature (including Aeschylus' *Agamemnon*, 1355,1365, etc., where it refers to the overthrow of the rightful king) and concludes that it cannot refer to Oedipus.

13 The idea of dignified old men dancing leads some (e.g., Dodds 1956: 46) to suggest that the chorus is stepping out of its role as character and asks this question as Athenian citizens. Dawe (2006: 186) is skeptical; Henrichs (1994) considers the question in the broader context of the play, i.e., as an index of the elders' dismay at Jocasta's repudiation of Apollo's oracles, but also as a query about the value of ritual dancing. He suggests that the elders' dancing is both situated in the immediate Theban context, but also in the physical place of their performance, "as if this chorus were dancing in Thebes as well as in Athens." He describes this phenomenon as "choral projection"(1994: 67–8).

14 Dawe (2006: 153) suggests a stone of Apollo Agyieus, the protector of the entrance to the house. Mastronarde (1994: 358) lists other instances when this prop would have been used in tragedy and discusses its possible appearance. The interior of a *kylix* (drinking cup) from the British Museum (BM1115.1) represents such an altar. See also Poe (1989: 136).

Chapter 4

1   The authenticity of *Rhesus* is disputed, but if genuine it would
    bring the number of complete plays to nineteen. These include
    the single entire specimen of a satyr play, *Cyclops*. I count
    Alcestis, considered to be "prosatyric," i.e., produced in place
    of a satyr drama at the end of the trilogy, among the tragedies
    for generic reasons. Dating of the plays is derived from external
    evidence, but more often from stylistic features.

2   Aristophanes' *Frogs* (405 BCE), which features a poetry contest
    between Euripides and Aeschylus in the afterlife, catalogues a
    list of how Euripides allegedly debased tragedy.

3   Whitman (1974: 35–7) observes in *Helen* a "complex
    dissonantal mingling of different points of view"; he does
    not dispute its tragic elements, but identifies a romantic tone.
    On the problematic concept of a tragic genre and Euripides'
    place within it, see Mastronarde (2010), who emphasizes the
    flexibility and versatility of the genre. Disputing any comic
    elements in *Helen*, Wright (2005: 28) observes: "neither
    Menelaus nor the portress is drunk, no one farts, no one suffers
    violence, and there is not a phallus in sight." Stavrinou (2014)
    presents a nuanced argument that the manipulation of scenic
    effects in Helen has affinities with comedy, which she describes
    as "inter-generic allusiveness."

4   See Allan (1999–2000) on Euripides' engagement with the
    Sophists in the context of war.

5   The language, as Allan notes, is "that of realistic portraiture"
    (2008: 158). Wohl (2015: 114) sums up the scholarship and
    notes: "The play's theme of illusion and reality is developed as
    a self-conscious metatheatricality, as Euripides reminds us again
    and again that the world of the play is just a dramatic fiction."

6   Aristophanes (e.g., *Acharnians* 412–34) mocks Euripides for
    featuring characters in rags, but Aeschylus has Xerxes arrive
    in rags in *Persians*. Whitman (1974: 46–9) connects Menelaus'
    clothing with the appearance-versus-reality theme.

7   Burian (2007: 38) notes the importance of costume in *Helen*,
    matched only by the *Bacchae*, which features the cross-dressing

male worshippers of Dionysus, Cadmus, and Tiresias, and then eventually Pentheus as well.

8   Holmberg (1995: 22–5) surveys and analyzes the development of the myth of Helen's phantom, which she observes is not incompatible with Homeric epics, even if they do not allude to it. She argues that even in the *Iliad* Helen is more "emblematic" than real; the Homeric warriors are fighting for a phantom.

9   Euripides' *Suppliant Women* features a different myth, but the emphasis is still on the appeal by Argive women for the intercession of Theseus to allow them to retrieve the bodies of their sons. Not all suppliant plays feature women: Tzanetou (2012) focuses on three plays (Aeschylus' *Eumenides*, Sophocles' *Oedipus at Colonus*, and Euripides' *Children of Heracles*) to demonstrate that the representation of Athens as a destination for the oppressed contributes to the self-fashioned notion of Athens as a protector of the oppressed.

10   In his study of the four plays (*Ion*, *IT*, *Helen*, and *Alcestis*) that feature a prediction in the prologue, Hamilton (1978: 278) observes that "the prediction is altered, questioned or contradicted in the course of the play," creating a tension in the audience about the fulfillment; inevitably the prophecy comes true, although not quite as expected.

11   Whitman (1974: 50) notes that the first half of the play is dominated by *tyche* ("chance"), while the second half is motivated by *techne* ("skill").

12   Seven lines of musical notation from the first stasimon of Euripides' *Orestes* (338–44) are preserved on a musical papyrus (Vienna G 2315) dating from the third century BCE. Marshall's synopsis (2014: 100–1) is useful.

13   Winged Sirens decorated grave monuments in Classical Greece, and according to the *Odyssey* (12.39–54), their songs lured sailors to their deaths. Burian (2007: 200–1) provides further context. Whitman (1974: 42) detects an allusion to Steisichorus' account of the phantom Helen.

14   In the parodos Helen contemplates suicide and then moves on to a compassionate lament for the pain and loss experienced by all female victims of the war. Helen's song also considers Zeus' intercourse in the form of a swan with her mother and

draws on exotic versions of other myths of seduction, including a strange vision of the nymph Callisto taking on the form of a bear before she climbs into bed with Zeus (330–85). The entire effect is a disorienting strangeness of myths that Helen herself only seems to half-believe, a spicy accent to a first episode that diverts the conventions with surprising flourishes.

15 Pickard-Cambridge (1968: 202) speculates that sleeved garments were necessary to hide the (male) actors' arms and possibly to keep them warm. Wyles (2011: 26–9, 40, 80) adduces contemporary vase paintings such as the Pronomos vase and discusses the practicalities of sewing these sleeved garments. Furthermore, she argues that sleeved garments, which were not worn by fifth-century Greeks, signified that the character was from the past.

16 Mastronarde (1990) provides a detailed analysis of all data regarding the *mechane*. Productions at smaller theaters outside of Athens, might not have had the crane; in such cases ladders behind the *skene* might achieve the desired effect.

BIBLIOGRAPHY

Allan, W. (ed. and comm.) (2008) *Euripides: Helen*, Cambridge: Cambridge University Press.

Arnott, P. (1962) *Greek Scenic Conventions in the Fifth Century B.C.*, Oxford: Clarendon Press.

Bain, D. (1977) *Actors and Audience: A Study of Asides and Related Conventions in Greek Drama*, Oxford: Oxford University Press.

Barker, E. (2009) *Entering the Agon. Dissent and Authority in Homer, Historiography, and Tragedy*, Oxford: Oxford University Press.

Blondell, R. (2002) *Sophocles: The Theban Plays*, Newburyport, MA: Focus Pub./R Pullins Co.

Boedeker, D. (2017) "Significant Inconsistencies in Euripides' *Helen*," in L. McClure (ed.), *The Wiley-Blackwell Companion to Euripides*, 243–57, Oxford: Wiley-Blackwell.

Boegehold, A. L. (1999) *When a Gesture Was Expected: A Selection of Examples from Archaic and Classical Greek Literature*, Princeton: Princeton University Press.

Braund, D., Hall, E., and Wyles, R. (2020) *Ancient Theatre and Performance Culture around the Black Sea*, Cambridge: Cambridge University Press.

Brøns, C. (2016) *Gods and Garments: Textiles in Greek Sanctuaries in the 7th to the 1st Centuries BC*, Oxford: Oxbow Books.

Burian, P. (1997) "Tragedy Adapted for Stages and Screens: the Renaissance to the Present," in P. E. Easterling (ed.), *The Cambridge Companion to Greek Tragedy*, 228–83, Cambridge: Cambridge University Press.

Burian, P. (2007) *Euripides, Helen*, Aris and Phillips Classical Texts, Oxford: Oxbow Books.

Burnett, A. P. (1971) *Catastrophe Survived: Euripides' Plays of Mixed Reversal*, Oxford: Oxford University Press.

Burns, K. (2020–1) "Leadership in the Time of COVID: Responding to Theater of War's *The Oedipus Project*," *Didaskalia*, 16.3, https://www.didaskalia.net/issues/16/3/, accessed February 5, 2021.

Carawan, E. (1999) "The Edict of Oedipus (*Oedipus Tyrannus* 223–51)," *American Journal of Philology*, 120: 187–222.

Carey, C. (1986) "The Second Stasimon of Sophocles' *Oedipus Tyrannus*," *Journal of Hellenic Studies*, 106: 175–9.

Collins, D. (2004) *Master of the Game: Competition and Performance in Greek Poetry*, Cambridge, MA: Harvard University Press.

Conacher, D. J. (1967) *Euripidean Drama: Myth, Theme and Structure*, Toronto: University of Toronto Press.

Conacher, D. J. (1998) *Euripides and the Sophists: Some Dramatic Treatments of Philosophical Ideas*, London: Duckworth.

Connelly, J. B. (2007) *Portrait of a Priestess: Women and Ritual in Ancient Greece*, Princeton: Princeton University Press.

Csapo, E. (2007) "The Men Who Built the Theatres: Theatropolai, Theatronai, and Arkhitektones," in P. Wilson (ed.), *The Greek Theatre and Festivals: Documentary Studies*, 87–115, Oxford: Oxford University Press.

Csapo, E. and Slater, W. (1994) *The Context of Ancient Drama*, Ann Arbor: University of Michigan Press.

Csapo, E. and Wilson, P. (2014) "Origins and History of Greek Tragedy," in H. Roisman (ed.), *The Encyclopedia of Greek Tragedy v. II*, 926–37, Oxford: Wiley-Blackwell.

Csapo, E. and Wilson, P. (2020) *A Social and Economic History of the Theatre to 300 BC. Vol. II. Theatre beyond Athens: Documents with Translation and Commentary*, Cambridge: Cambridge University Press.

Csapo, E., Goette, H. R., Green, J. R., and Wilson, P. (2014) *Greek Theatre in the Fourth Century BC*, Berlin: De Gruyter.

Dawe, R. D. (2006) *Sophocles: Oedipus Rex*, Cambridge: Cambridge University Press.

De Romilly, J. (1958) *La crainte et l'angoisse dans le théatre d'Eschyle*, Paris: Les Belles Lettres.

Dillon, M. (2002) *Girls and Women in Classical Greek Religion*, London and New York: Routledge.

Dunn, F. M. (2007) *Present Shock in Late Fifth Century Greece*, Ann Arbor: University of Michigan Press.

Dunn, F. M. (1995) *Tragedy's End: Closure and Innovation in Euripidean Drama*, Oxford: Oxford University Press.

Edmonds, L. (1985) *Oedipus: The Ancient Legend and Its Later Analogues*, Baltimore and London: The Johns Hopkins University Press.

Esposito, S. (1996) "The Changing Roles of the Sophoclean Chorus," *Arion*, 4: 85–114.

Fletcher, J. (1999) "Choral Voice and Narrative in the First Stasimon of Aeschylus' *Agamemnon*," *Phoenix*, 53: 29–49.

Fletcher, J. (2007) "The Virgin Choruses of Aeschylus," in B. MacLachlan and J. Fletcher (eds), *Virginity Revisited: Configurations of the Unpossessed Body*, 24–39, Toronto: University of Toronto Press.

Fletcher, J. (2012) *Performing Oaths in Classical Greek Drama*, Cambridge: Cambridge University Press.

Fletcher, J. (2014) "Polyphony to Silence: The Jurors of the *Oresteia*," *College Literature*, 41: 56–75.

Foley, H. P. (2001) *Female Acts in Greek Tragedy*, Princeton: Princeton University Press.

Foley, H. P. (2003) "Choral Identity in Greek Tragedy," *Classical Philology*, 98: 1–30.

Garland, R. (2004) *Surviving Greek Tragedy*, Ann Arbor: University of Michigan Press.

Garvie, A. F. (2006) *Aeschylus' Supplices: Play and Trilogy,* 2nd ed., Cambridge: Cambridge University Press.

Garvie, A. F. (2008) *Aeschylus: Persae: With Introduction and Commentary*, Oxford: Oxford University Press.

Goette, H. R. (2007) "The Archaeology of the 'Rural' Dionysia in Attica," in E. Csapo, H. R. Goette, J. R. Green, and P. Wilson (eds), 77–106, *Greek Theatre in the Fourth Century BC*, Berlin: De Gruyter.

Goldhill, S. (1996) "Collectivity and Otherness: The Authority of the Tragic Chorus," in M. S. Silk (ed.), *Tragedy and the Tragic: Greek Theatre and Beyond*, 244–56, Oxford: Oxford University Press.

Goward, B. (1999) *Tragedy. Narrative Technique in Aeschylus, Sophocles and Euripides*, London: Bloomsbury Academic.

Green, J. R. (1991) "Seeing and Depicting the Theatre in Classical Athens," *Greek, Roman, and Byzantine Studies*, 32: 15–50.

Green, J. R. (1994) *Theatre in Ancient Greek Society*, London and New York: Routledge.

Griffith, D. (1996) *Theatre of Apollo: Divine Justice and Sophocles' Oedipus the King*, Montreal: McGill Queens University Press.

Griffith, M. (2002) "Slaves of Dionysos: Satyrs, Audience, and the Ends of the *Oresteia*," *Classical Antiquity*, 21: 195–258.

Hall, E. (1998) "Ithyphallic Males Behaving Badly, or, Satyr Drama as Gendered Tragic Ending," in M. Wyke (ed.), *Parchments of Gender: Deciphering the Bodies of Antiquity*, 13–37, Oxford: Oxford University Press.

Hall, E. (2002) "The Singing Actors of Antiquity," in P. E. Easterling and E. Hall (eds), *Greek and Roman Actors: Aspects of an Ancient Profession*, 3–38, Cambridge: Cambridge University Press.

Hamilton, R. (1978) "Prologue Prophecy and Plot in Four Plays of Euripides," *American Journal of Philology*, 99: 277–302.

Hamilton, R. (1985) "Euripidean Priests," *Harvard Studies in Classical Philology*, 89: 53–73.

Harris, E. (2010) "Is Oedipus Guilty? Sophocles and Athenian Homicide Law," in E. Harris, D. F. Leão, and P. J. Rhodes (eds), *Law and Drama in Ancient Greece*, 122–46, London: Bloomsbury Academic.

Hecht, A. and Bacon, H. (1973) *Seven Against Thebes*, Oxford: Oxford University Press.

Henderson, J. (2007) "Drama and Democracy," in L. J. Samons II (ed.), *The Cambridge Companion to the Age of Pericles*, 179–95, Cambridge: Cambridge University Press.

Henrichs, A. (1994) "Why Should I Dance?" Choral Self-Referentiality in Greek Tragedy," *Arion*, 3: 56–111.

Holmberg, I. E. (1995) "Euripides' *Helen*: Most Noble and Most Chaste," *American Journal of Philology*, 116: 19–42.

Hutchinson, G. O. (1985) *Aeschylus: Seven Against Thebes*: *Introduction and Commentary*, Oxford: Clarendon Press.

Jackson, L. (2020) *The Chorus of Drama in the Fourth Century BCE: Presence and Representation*, Oxford: Oxford University Press.

Kaimio, M. (1988) *Physical Contact in Greek Tragedy: A Study of Stage Conventions*, Helsinki: Suomalainen Tiedeakatemia.

Karanika, A. (2014) *Voices at Work: Women, Performance, and Labor in Ancient Greece*, Baltimore: Johns Hopkins University Press.

Kirkwood, G. (1955) *A Study of Sophoclean Drama*, Ithaca: Cornell University Press.

Knox, B. (1972) "Aeschylus and the Third Actor," *American Journal of Philology*, 93: 104–23.

Knox, B. (1975) *Oedipus at Thebes*: Sophocles' *Tragic Hero and His Time*, New Haven: Yale University Press.

Konstantinou, A. (2018) *Female Mobility and Gendered Space in Ancient Greek Myth*, London and New York: Bloomsbury.

Kovacs, D. (2009) "The Role of Apollo in *Oedipus Tyrannus*," in J. R. C. Cousland and J. R. Hume (eds), *The Play of Texts and Fragments: Essays in Honour of Martin Cropp*, 357–68, Leiden: Brill.

Kowalzig, B. (2016) "Transcultural Chorality: *Iphigenia in Tauris* and Athenian Imperial Economics in a Polytheistic World," in R. Gagné and M. Hopman (eds), *Choral Mediations in Greek Drama*, 178–210, Cambridge: Cambridge University Press.

Lamari, A. (2017) *Reperforming Greek Tragedy: Theater, Politics, and Cultural Mobility in the Fifth and Fourth Centuries BC*, Berlin and Boston: De Gruyter.

Lateiner, D. (2014) "Proxemics," in H. Roisman (ed.), *The Encyclopedia of Greek Tragedy v. II*, 1023–5, Oxford: Wiley-Blackwell.

Lefkowitz, M. (1981) *The Lives of the Greek Poets*, Baltimore: Johns Hopkins University Press.

Lewis, D. (1955) "Who Was Lysistrata?" *Annual of the British School at Athens*, 50: 1–12.

Ley, G. (2007) *The Theatricality of Greek Tragedy*: *Playing Space and Chorus*, Chicago: University of Chicago Press.

Liapis, V. (2012) *A Commentary on the Rhesus Attributed to Euripides*, Oxford: Oxford University Press.

Loraux, N. (1987) *Tragic Ways of Killing a Woman*, Cambridge, MA: Harvard University Press.

Marshall, C. W. (1999) "Some Fifth-Century Masking Conventions," *Greece & Rome*, 46: 188–202.

Marshall, C. W. (2014) *The Structure and Performance of Euripides' Helen*, Cambridge: Cambridge University Press.

Marshall, C. W. and van Willigenburg, S. (2004) "Judging Athenian Dramatic Competitions," *Journal of Hellenic Studies*, 124: 90–107.

Mastronarde, D. (2010) *The Art of Euripides. Dramatic Technique and Social Context*, Cambridge: Cambridge University Press.

Matthiessen, K. (1968) "Zur Theonoeszene der Euripideischen Helena," *Hermes*, 96: 685–704.

McAuley, G. (2000) *Space in Performance: Making Meaning in the Theatre*, Ann Arbor: University of Michigan Press.

McClure, L. (1999) *Spoken Like a Woman*: *Speech and Gender in Athenian Drama*, Princeton: Princeton University Press.

McClure, L. (2016) "Priestess and Polis in Euripides' *Iphigeneia in Tauris*," in M. Dillon, E. Eidinow, and L. Maurizio (eds), *Women's Ritual Competence in the Greco-Roman Mediterranean*, 115–30, London and New York: Routledge.

Meineck, P. (2014) "Masks," in H. Roisman (ed.), *The Encyclopedia of Greek Tragedy v. II*, 800–2, Oxford: Wiley-Blackwell.

Mikalson, J. (1991) *Honor Thy Gods: Popular Religion in Greek Tragedy*, Chapel Hill: University of North Carolina Press.

Mitchell-Boyask, R. (2008) *Plague and the Athenian Imagination: Drama, History, and the Cult of Asclepius*, Cambridge: Cambridge University Press.

Mueller, M. (2016) *Objects as Actors: Props and the Poetics of Performance in Greek Tragedy*, Chicago: University of Chicago Press.

Murnaghan, S. (2016) "The Choral Plot of Euripides' *Helen*," in R. Gagné and M. Hopman (eds.), *Choral Mediations in Greek Drama*, 155–77, Cambridge: Cambridge University Press.

Nooter, S. (2017) *The Mortal Voice in the Tragedies of Aeschylus*, Cambridge: Cambridge University Press.

Ormand, K. (1996) "Silent by Convention? Sophocles' Tekmessa," *American Journal of Philology*, 117: 37–64.

Ormand, K. (2003) "Oedipus the Queen: Cross-Gendering without Drag," *Theatre Journal*, 55: 1–28.

O'Higgins, D. (2007) *Women and Humor in Classical Greece*, Cambridge: Cambridge University Press.

Padel, R. (1974) "'Imagery of the Elsewhere': Two Choral Odes of Euripides," *Classical Quarterly*, 24: 227–41.

Pickard-Cambridge, A. (1966) *The Theatre of Dionysus in Athens*, Oxford: Oxford University Press.

Pickard-Cambridge, A. (1968) *The Dramatic Festivals of Athens*, 2nd ed., Oxford: Clarendon Press.

Podlecki, A. P. (2005) "Aischylos Satyrikos," in G. W. M. Harrison and Z. P. Ambrose (eds), *Satyr Drama: Tragedy at Play*, 1–19, Swansea: Classical Press of Wales.

Poe, J. (1989) "The Altar in the Fifth-century Theater," *Classical Philology*, 8: 116–39.

Poochigian, A. (2007) "Arguments from Silence: Text and Stage in Aischylos' *Seven Against Thebes*," *Classical Journal*, 103: 1–11.

Rabinowitz, N. (1993) *Anxiety Veiled: Euripides and the Traffic in Women*, Ithaca: Cornell University Press.

Rehm, R. (1994) *Marriage to Death: The Conflation of Wedding and Funeral Rituals in Greek Tragedy*, Princeton: Princeton University Press.

Rehm, R. (2002) *The Play of Space*: *Spatial Transformation in Greek Tragedy*, Princeton: Princeton University Press.

Ringer, M. (2016) *Euripides and the Boundaries of the Human*, Lanham, MD: Lexington Books.

Roselli, D. (2011) *Theater of the People: Spectators and Society in Ancient Athens*, Austin, TX: University of Texas Press.

Sansone, D. (1975) "The Third Stasimon of the *Oedipus Tyrannos*," *Classical Philology*, 70: 110–17.

Sansone, D. (2016) "The Size of the Tragic Chorus," *Phoenix*, 70: 233–54.

Schechner, R. (1977) *Essays on Performance Theory 1970–76*, New York: Drama Book Specialists.

Schlegel, A. W. (1846) *Vorlesungen über dramatische Kunst und Literatur 1*, Vienna: C.F. Schade. [Translated by John Black under the title *Course of Lectures on Dramatic Art and Literature* (New York, 1973).]

Scodel, R. (1982) "*Hybris* in the Second Stasimon of the *Oedipus Rex*," *Classical Philology*, 77: 214–23.

Scott, W. (1996) *Musical Design* in *Sophoclean Theater*, Hanover, NH: University Press of New England.

Seale, D. (1983) *Vision and Stagecraft in Sophocles*, London: Croom Helm.

Segal, C. P. (1971) "The Two Worlds of Euripides' *Helen*," *Transactions of the American Philological Association*, 102: 553–61.

Segal, C. P. (1981) *Tragedy and Civilization*: *An Interpretation of Sophocles*, Cambridge, MA: Harvard University Press.

Sewell-Rutter, N. J. (2007) *Guilt by Descent: Moral Inheritance and Decision Making in Greek Tragedy*, Oxford: Oxford University Press.

Sidwell, K. (1992) "The Argument of the Second Stasimon of *Oedipus Tyrannus*," *Journal of Hellenic Studies*, 112: 106–22.

Sifakis, G. M. (2013) "The Misunderstanding of *Opsis* in Aristotle's *Poetics*," in G. W. M. Harrison and V. Liapis (eds), *Performance in Greek and Roman Theater*, 45–62, Leiden and Boston: Brill.

Sofer, A. (2003) *The Stage Life of Props*, Ann Arbor: University of Michigan Press.

Sofer, A. (2013) *Dark Matter*: *Invisibility in Drama, Theater, and Performance*, Ann Arbor: University of Michigan Press.

Solmsen, F. (1937) "The Erinys in Aischylos *Septem*," *Transactions of the American Philological Association*, 68: 97–211.

Sommerstein, A. H. (2010) *Aeschylean Tragedy*, London: Duckworth.

Sommerstein, A. H. (2011) "Sophocles and the Guilt of Oedipus," *Estudios Griegos e Indoeuropeos*, 21: 93–107.

Sourvinou-Inwood, C. (1990) "What Is Polis Religion?" in O. Murray and S. Price (eds), *The Greek City from Homer to Alexander*, 295–322, Oxford: Oxford University Press.

Sourvinou-Inwood, C. (2000) "Further Aspects of Polis Religion," in R. Buxton (ed.), *Oxford Readings in Greek Religion*, 38–55, Oxford: Oxford University Press.

Sourvinou-Inwood, C. (2003) *Tragedy and Athenian Religion*, Lanham: Lexington Books.

Stanford, W. B. (1963) *Sophocles, Ajax. Edited with Introduction, Revised Text, Commentary, Appendixes, Indexes*, London: McMillan.

Stavrinou, A. S. (2015) "The *opsis* of *Helen*: Performative Intertextuality in Euripides' Helen," *Greek, Roman and Byzantine Studies*, 55: 104–32.

Stehle, E. (2005) "Prayer and Curse in Aeschylus' *Seven Against Thebes*," *Classical Philology*, 100: 101–22.

Steiner, D. (2011) "Dancing with the Stars: *Choreia* in the Third Stasimon of Euripides' *Helen*," *Classical Antiquity*, 106: 299–323.

Stewart, E. (2017) *Greek Tragedy on the Move: The Birth of a Panhellenic Art Form c. 500–300 BC*, Oxford: Oxford University Press.

Swift, L. (2010) *The Hidden Chorus: Echoes of Genre in Tragic Lyric*, Oxford: Oxford University Press.

Taplin, O. (1977) *The Stagecraft of Aeschylus*, Oxford: Oxford University Press.

Taplin, O. (1978) *Greek Tragedy in Action*, Oxford: Oxford University Press.

Taplin, O. (2007) *Pots & Plays: Interactions between Tragedy and Greek Vase-painting of the Fourth Century B.C.*, Los Angeles: J. Paul Getty Museum.

Thalmann, W. (1978) *Dramatic Art in Aeschylus's Seven Against Thebes*, New Haven: Yale University Press.

Torrance, I. (2013) *Metapoetry in Euripides*, Oxford: Oxford University Press.

Torres-Guerra, J. (2015) "Thebaid," in M. Fantuzzi and C. Tsagalis (eds), *The Greek Epic Cycle and Its Ancient Reception: A Companion*, 226–43, Cambridge: Cambridge University Press.

Tzanetou, A. (2012) *City of Suppliants: Tragedy and the Athenian Empire*, Austin: University of Texas.

Versnel, H. S. (1990) *Inconsistencies in Greek Religion, 1. Ter Unus: Isis, Dionysus, Hermes. Three Studies in Henotheism*, Leiden: Brill.

Weiberg, E. (2020) "The Bed and the Tomb: The Materiality of Signs in Euripides," *Mnemosyne*, 73: 729–49.

Weiss, N. A. (2018) *The Music of Tragedy: Performance and Imagination in Euripidean Theater*, Oakland: University of California Press.

West, M. L. (1989) "The Early Chronology of Attic Tragedy," *Classical Quarterly*, 39: 251–4.

Whitman, C. H. (1974) *Euripides and the Full Circle of Myth*, Cambridge, MA: Harvard University Press.

Wiles, D. (1993) "The Seven Gates of Aeschylus," in N. W. Slater and B. Zimmermann (eds), *Intertextualität in der griechischrömischen Komödie*, 180–94, Stuttgart: Springer-Verlag.

Wiles, D. (2007) *Mask and Performance in Greek Tragedy: From Ancient Festival to Modern Experimentation*, Cambridge: Cambridge University Press.

Wilson, P. (2000) *The Athenian Institution of the Khoregia. The Chorus, the City and the Stage*, Cambridge: Cambridge University Press.

Winkler, J. J. (1990) "The Ephebes' Song: Tragoidia and Polis," in J. J. Winkler and F. Zeitlin (eds), *Nothing to Do with Dionysus? Athenian Drama in Its Social Context*, 20–62, Princeton: Princeton University Press.

Wohl, V. (2015) *Euripides* and the *Politics of Form*, Princeton: Princeton University Press.

Wolff, C. (1973) "On Euripides' *Helen*," *Harvard Studies in Classical Philology*, 77: 61–84.

Wright, M. (2005) *Euripides' Escape-Tragedies: A Study of Helen, Andromeda, and Iphigenia among the Taurians*, Oxford: Oxford University Press.

Wright, M. (2016) *The Lost Plays of Greek Tragedy (Volume 1): Neglected Authors*, London and New York: Bloomsbury Academic.

Wyles, R. (2011) *Costume in Greek Tragedy*, London: Bristol Classical Press.

Xanthakis-Karamanos, G. (1980) *Studies in Fourth Century Tragedy*, Athens: Academy of Athens.

Zeitlin, F. I. (1978) "The Dynamics of Misogyny: Myth and Mythmaking in the *Oresteia*," *Arethusa* (Women in the Ancient World), 11: 149–84.

Zeitlin, F. I. (1982) *Under the Sign of the Shield. Semiotics and Aeschylus' Seven Against Thebes*, Rome: Edizioni dell'Ateneo.

Zeitlin, F. I. (1990) "Theater and Self and Society in Athenian Drama," in J. Winkler and F. Zeitlin (eds), *Nothing to Do with Dionysus? Athenian Drama in Its Social Context*, 130–67, Princeton: Princeton University Press.

Zweig, B. (1999) "Euripides' *Helen* and Female Rites of Passage," in M. Padilla (ed.), *Rites of Passage in Ancient Greece*, 158–80, Lewisburg: Bucknell University Press.

INDEX